MARKETING YOUR WEBSITE

GW00692137

For a complete list of Management Books 2000 titles,
visit our web-site on http://www.mb2000.com

MARKETING YOUR WEBSITE

Laurel Alexander

2000

First published in 2002 by Management Books 2000 Ltd
Forge House, Limes Road
Kemble, Cirencester
Gloucestershire, GL7 6AD, UK
Tel: 0044 (0) 1285 771441/2
Fax: 0044 (0) 1285 771055
E-mail: m.b.2000@virgin.net
Web: mb2000.com

Printed and bound in Great Britain by Biddles, Guildford

British Library Cataloguing in Publication Data is available
ISBN 1-85252-392-1

Contents

Preface

I know half of my advertising is wasted. I just don't know which half!
John Wanamaker
Department store pioneer and advertising prophet

So, you have the best product or service since sliced bread. You have a website ready to sell to the gagging punters. But no one is buying. Is anyone even visiting? Whoops – have we got another dot.bomb? No matter how fantastic your product or service, if you don't get your marketing strategy right – your bank account will stay very empty! This book can't tell you how to get rich quick (let me know if you find out), but it can help you get your website marketing act together so that you have a better chance of buying that villa on the Costa del Wherever.

So what marketing promotions do you start first for the biggest profit? Once you have submitted your site to the search engines and started to communicate with other sites to get reciprocal links, you want to focus your time on email discussion lists, ezines, newsgroups, bulletin boards/classified ads, mailing lists and commercial online services to get immediate cash flow. These are instant marketing tools that will generate income in a matter of days allowing you to test ads, slogans, salesletters, and your website design to get a winning combination before you really start to get traffic from reciprocal links and search engine listings.

You must have an organic marketing plan right from the beginning which develops in response to market forces. If you have a good front-end (your main product or service), as your business starts to grow, you can be implementing your back-end products and services (sales made after the client has first bought from you) as this is where the real money is. Get your website marketing right and the bank manager will being coming to you for a loan.

Good luck with your dot.com!

Laurel Alexander   **laurelalexander@pavilion.co.uk**

1

Overview of E-marketing

CLICK-ONS
Planning the buy
Creating a corporate ID
Using a psychological marketing plan
Creating an online image
Offline moving online
Defining the online customer
Six steps for internet marketing

Nearly 4 million UK homes have plugged into the internet during the past year, bringing the number of online-homes in the UK to 10 million (up from 6 million in May 2000). The study conducted by the Office of Telecommunications (Oftel) in May 2001, also found 24 percent of the households in Britain were connected to the internet via fully unmetered products, compared with 18 percent in the same period of 2000. The research also found the number of adults online has eclipsed the number of teens online, growing 18 percent from April 2000 to April 2001.

E-commerce has flourished on the internet. But no matter how fantastic your product or service, you are going to sink like a thousand dot-bombs have already, if you don't get your e-marketing strategy right. But getting the strategy right means you have to keep working at your marketing, evaluating outcomes and improving that strategy.

Planning the buy

So you have a service or a product to sell and you have decided that the world wide web can offer unlimited market potential. Where do you start your e-marketing campaign?

If you're trying to talk to people about a brand of coffee, for example, when is the best time to do that? Morning? Noon? Late night? And since the product you're interested in talking to them about is bought at the supermarket, what days are they most likely to be going to the supermarket to shop? Do they get in their cars Monday night to go to the supermarket, or is it Friday, right before the weekend? Much of the ad-serving technology available today can allow for a wide variety of targeting so that ads can be served to a certain demographic on a certain day at a certain time. Here are three target-related issues to consider when planning your e-marketing strategy:

- **Time-of-day flighting**. In broadcast media, inventory is purchased by 'daypart' (a certain time block during a 24-hour period). Overnight dayparts (which are not even measured by ratings) are much less expensive than, say, prime time (8pm to 11pm). But on the web, you're paying the same price for inventory whether it's 4pm or 4am. Again, as with **day-of-week flighting**, you can improve the efficiency of all impressions run, regardless of the direct response or the correlative action instigated.
- **Frequency control**. If your interest is the click-through rate, frequency is still one of the most important things you can do. Research suggests that between 80 and 90 percent of all clicks on ads happen on the first exposure to an ad unit, e.g. banners. By limiting your frequency to one or two ad units, you will increase the efficiency of your campaign by dropping what are essentially ineffectual impressions.
- **Day-of-week flighting**. It will be necessary to first run a test buy before figuring out which days are most active and appropriate for your product. But once you do, this can be another way to increase the efficiency of the direct responses you get as well as the possible relevance quality of the impression that makes an impression and leads to correlative activity.

The key selling steps

Selling is worlds away from allowing customers to buy, and if you aren't selling, you're not going to be in business for long. If you want your web site to sell more, you have to construct it in such a way that it employs these key selling processes:

- You arouse potential customers' interest, and once you've brought them to your site, the first thing you do is reinforce that they're in the right place by presenting your unique selling proposition (USP).
- The process of building rapport online, where you lack that nose-to-nose (N2N) element, is simple. You develop rapport through things such as the speed of your download and the professional appearance of your site; through elements that promote trust; through ease of navigation, the power of your text, and the relevance of your images; and through exceptional customer service. You make no assumptions about the customer's prior knowledge, either about computers or products. You offer clear access to help and provide concise, relevant information. You also understand that there are different personality types and people have their particular way of shopping. You use that information to adapt your sales process to the individual, and you sell to customers in the way they want to be sold to.
- A key ingredient of eventually closing the sale is doing the qualifying part right. Discovering exactly what your prospect really wants is your biggest challenge. So you begin a dialogue with your prospect. How do you ask questions? They're implicit in which hyperlinks you choose to provide. In general there are three types of buyers: those who know exactly want they want, those who know generally what they want, and those who are browsing and need some direction. You need navigation and information architecture that addresses the needs of all.
- Now you must begin to close the sale by communicating. You answer the prospect's questions, resolve objections, encourage the close, detail service plans, offer payment options, and explain your guarantees. And you communicate not just any place but specifically at the point of action (POA), where it matters most to your prospect that you stand behind your products and care about his or her security and privacy. You create trust and confidence, a sense that he or she will not be forgotten the second the transaction is consummated.

The information architecture of your web site must recognise every step of these key sales processes. Remember, too, that each step feeds the others, so it's not unusual to have two, three, or even all five steps on a single page.

Think of the process as operating on a micro level and a macro level simultaneously: the micro level is the individual page; the macro level is the entire shopping and buying experience. And always remember, buying is ultimately an emotions-based process. By following these steps and applying these processes, you not only engage your shoppers in the physical dimension of colours, shapes, sizes, and prices, but also connect to the critical emotional and psychological dimensions that underlie every decision to buy.

UK web ad market subject to problems

A new online advertising study in the UK says new media advertising formats will become an important part of all major integrated media campaigns in the coming years. However, according to Allegra Strategies, a number of factors limit current uptake of the medium, and may lead to a small decline in UK online ad revenues. Allegra says that in order to establish itself as a valid mainstream advertising medium, the industry needs to ensure the adoption of established marketing principles, set and manage realistic expectations, and act responsibly to gain consumers' consent-to-market.

Marketing the niche

How can you make your website stand out? The best way to attract visitors to your website and keep them coming back is to be the best (or only) website out there doing what you're doing. A niche is a community of people. They can be fans of a particular sport, hobbyists or business people. The point is, this community has common needs. You can speak specifically to them, and offer information and services not available elsewhere. You might even have an opportunity to build a place for the community to meet online. Since you're focusing all your marketing resources on one group of people, you can find places where you can reach more of them for less money. You don't have to worry about the added cost of offering a diverse product line. Plus, since you offer more value than your competition, you can charge a premium for your product, which means you don't have to worry about having the lowest prices on the net!

The Unique Selling Proposition (USP)

In developing your marketing message, it's very helpful to develop a Unique Selling Proposition (USP). The USP answers the question, 'Why should I do business with you instead of your competitors?' There are two major benefits in developing the USP. First, it clearly differentiates your business in the eyes of your current and potential customers or clients. Second, it focuses you (and your team) on delivering the promise of the USP, helping to improve your internal performance. It should be tested to assure the USP addresses a need that is truly important to the buyer.

Are you directing 100% of your marketing effort at 15% of your audience?

For most businesses, half of the customers already know what they are going to buy and where they are going to buy it. Another 35% of their customers will come by referral from another customer. That leaves only 15 out of a hundred customers coming from the 'cold marketplace,' yet most businesses direct almost all of their marketing efforts at the cold market. In direct marketing, when you mail or direct your efforts to a list that you don't have a previous relationship with, you are fortunate to get a 2% response. The response to most direct mailings is less than one percent. When you mail an offer that matches the desires of your 'house list,' with which you have established a relationship, response rates of more than 20% aren't unusual. The moral of the story? In order to increase the effectiveness of your marketing efforts, focus on doing more business with your existing customers.

Interview with marketing guru Craig Forté by Joe Polish

The 10-30-60 marketing rule

The 10-30-60 marketing rule says to spend 10% of your ad budget on untargeted marketing. Your ads should be aimed at everyone. The idea is to do a broad sweep across the public to find a few people who will become interested prospects. Spend 30% of your budget on interested prospects. This is targeted advertising to specific opt-in lists, postcards to certain people in your industry, and mailings to people who have called or emailed for more information. Finally, spend 60% on current and previous customers. People who have already bought from you are by far the most likely to buy again.

Creating a corporate ID

Next to naming a company, creating a corporate identity can stir emotions more than anything else you will do in the early planning stages of your company. Your company name and logo speak volumes to the outside world. Your logo should be a statement of who you are and what you are all about as an organisation. More and more, the company name and corporate identity are part of a larger brand-building process. Here are some tips on developing a process that will generate the best long-term results for your company:

- The first step before you embark on your corporate identity development is to develop your company's brand strategy and target audience profiling.
- The next step is to translate all that information into your logo design. Ask yourself whether you want your company to be perceived as big and traditional or modern and eclectic, technology or service driven, or serious or fun. Whatever your answers, they need to be conveyed in your logo design. Create a multidimensional logo. One of the biggest mistakes companies make in logo development is that the logos can be used only one-dimensionally. In other words, the logo looks good on a business card, but that's about it. Either the colours are too thin, the types too light, or the logo just doesn't transfer well when you shrink it or place it on a home page. The best logos work everywhere and anywhere.
- Avoid design clichés. Swooshes, ellipses, and little running men are just some of the many design clichés that people rely on to convey a company's brand. And while these tools are familiar and comfortable, they are mainstream and do not stand out in today's competitive landscape.
- Don't date your design. Just as you should choose for your company a name that won't embarrass you down the road, design your logo with an eye on the future. If you make your logo timeless, people will always relate to it. And while it may be tempting to go with the trendy colours and typefaces of a particular time, keep in mind that they will quickly look dated, along with your company.

Using a psychological marketing plan

If your marketing plan is not anchored firmly in the psychology of your customers' buying behaviour, you are vulnerable because your competitors who understand psychological marketing will use it to take market share away from you! To understand psychological marketing, you must first understand this:

People do not want your product or service. They want answers to problems, solutions to needs, pathways to wants, or a secret door to their heart's desires. But they don't want to give you their money to get it. So why do they pay you? That answer is inside the buyer's mind. The more precisely you know their real reasons for buying, the more precisely you can focus your marketing plan, and the more sales you will make.

The company that understands the most about the true buying motivations of its customers can dominate its industry with a good product or service and a focused marketing strategy.

A psychological profile of the targeted potential customer base and the product or service forms the foundation of an effective marketing plan. Every marketing decision flows naturally from the customer psychological profile – your advertising, promotions, public relations, packaging etc. Your psychological marketing plan focuses on your buyer's mind. You look out through his/her eyes at your product or service. There are four types of psychological hot spots that motivate your customers to buy:

Needs   Wants   Fears   Desires

People buy the 'promise of satisfaction'. The foundation of your psychological marketing plan is anchored in these four types of satisfactions:

NEEDS – The basic things that you think you must have, e.g. if you're hungry, you need food or if you're sick, you need medicine.

WANTS – These are things, which you would like, but which aren't really necessary, you can get along without them, e.g. a cream cake or new car seat covers. It is important to recognise the difference between your buyer's 'needs' and 'wants.' Each requires a different advertising and marketing approach.

FEARS – These are things, which we do not want to happen. Fears help us make wise decisions by considering negative possibilities, such as 'Can I afford it?' or 'Will it do the job?' Fears hold us back. A buyer balances needs, wants and desires against fears in making the final buying decision. That is why a psychological marketing plan always takes a buyer's fears into account. There are two categories of fears to take into account in your plans: The customer's fear of the status quo, e.g. 'if I don't get this tear in my shirt fixed, it will just get worse' is one of the reasons he/she is interested in your product or service. Obviously, you should try to stimulate that fear when you are designing your marketing message. The second kind of fear is that of making a mistake in choosing a solution to the problem, e.g. 'I could take my shirt to Blogg's Cleaners, but how do I know they will do a good job? They might ruin my favourite shirt.' These types of fears must be taken into account by offering reassurances to the customer that your company can satisfy his expectations.

DESIRES – These are like daydreams e.g. romance, wealth, or happiness. Winning the lottery is a desire, as is making every traffic light green on the drive to work. Desires are seldom met, but they are powerful motivators.

What are you really selling?
You may think you're selling kitchen units, training packs or cheese. Gillette knows that it doesn't sell blades. It sells clean shaves. Revlon knows it doesn't sell nail polish. It sells romance. Every product or service has at least one powerful motivator, which can be used to seduce buyers into parting with their money in return for 'Satisfying the Dream'. But your psychological marketing plan can only succeed if you identify your customers' exact, inner motivations and the way your product or service can satisfy them. Remember – people don't buy your product or service because they want it, but because they think it will satisfy some of their needs, wants, fears, or desires.

Creating an online image

When it comes to the internet, projecting a professional image is essential. How your website looks and reads will determine whether visitors stop to look around and tell their contacts how great your site is.

Professional text
You need to include some text on every page of your website to explain where visitors are and what they should do. Elements of professional text include:

- **Perfect spelling** – spell-check all your web pages, no matter how good a speller you think you are. If there is just one surprise, your visitors will lose confidence in you.
- **Perfect grammar** – grammar checks aren't perfect, so you may want someone with good grammar skills to check your website. If you don't have one, use the grammar check.
- **Good layout** – use plenty of white space, and a maximum of two font styles (one for headings and one for everything else). Make your paragraphs short and use subheadings and bullets to break up large sections of text.
- **Being convincing** – list the benefits of your website and the products or services you offer as well as describing them. Let some of your personality and enthusiasm creep into your text.

Professional graphics

Your graphics are the first thing your visitors will see when they come to your website. They must look nice and emphasise the best parts of each page. Some tips include:

- All your graphics must look good, even if it's supposed to look like a five-year-old drew it. Have other people critique your graphics, if you're designing them yourself. If you aren't graphically inclined, consider hiring a professional to create a few unique graphics for your website. You can use clip-art buttons and bullets, but your website should use more than just clip-art graphics.
- Animation can make your site look great, but use it sparingly. Ideally, an animation should emphasise the most important part of your website e.g. buy me!, subscribe now!
- If you have large graphics or a lot of them, make sure they are all as small a file size as possible to reduce your page load time.
- Choose one set of colours to use throughout your website, and make sure they look good on all platforms. Tip: There is a palette of 216 web safe colours. Use them!

Professional background

Use a light coloured background. If you must have a pattern, make sure it is subtle. Stay away from busy background images which can distract from your message, not to mention making your website difficult to read.

Bells and whistles

Streaming audio and video, complicated animations, nested tables, and Javascript can bog your page down. The more you add, the longer it will take visitors to download your page. Use them sparingly, and make sure your visitors can turn them off. Keep in mind that your visitors are often impatient and leave after waiting 30 seconds or so for your page to download. They may have slower modems and/or older browsers to wrestle with. You should keep your webpages' loading as quickly as possible. One way to use sound and video without keeping visitors waiting is to offer a link to them from your main webpage. When adding bells and whistles, always remember to ask yourself the following:

- How much will this add to my load time?
- Would this be less effective if I made it accessible by a link instead?
- How much will this add to my visitor's experience?

Offline moving online

'The dot.com tide has begun to ebb.' Those were the words of Forrester analyst Jim Nail in a January 2001 report that predicted dot.coms share of online advertising spending would shrink from 69 percent in 2000 to 16 percent in 2005. True to Nail's words, Nielsen//NetRatings reported in March that dot-coms were falling from the ranks of online advertisers, with just 34 'digital economy' companies listed among the top 100 online advertisers. The flipside of Nail's prediction is that the other 84 percent of online advertising spending will come from not.coms, or traditional, mainstream advertisers with established brands and budgets. It's these offline advertisers that can help the internet reach its full potential as an advertising medium by avoiding the missteps of the dot.com burnouts. Offline advertisers that are starting to consider the web in their marketing mix need to note the following:

Make your advertising goal-oriented

All online advertising should be focused on performance. Tying your online ads to specific goals is important for two reasons. First, it makes the creative in your ads more effective. The problem with many banner ads is that they just try to grab the consumer's attention so they will click on the ad. But the ads don't tell the consumer what they'll get when they click. Performance-based ads require a strong call to action, and therefore elicit better response. Second, pay-for-performance ads are more cost efficient.

Don't waste money branding online

Offline advertisers are fortunate in that they don't have to build their brand in order to sell online. Instead, they can draw on existing relationships with customers that were initiated offline. According to a study by the market intelligence firm NPD Group, search listings work better than standard banners with regard to brand recall or favourable opinion ratings. And they're less expensive than banner ads priced on a CPM basis. In fact, there are even search providers such as GoTo.com that operate on a pay-for-performance basis.

Defining the online customer

Marketers must find a way to bring clarity to the picture of the online customer. Customer behaviour is evolving overall, and is beginning to differ according to experience, gender, and demographics. Additionally, people behave differently at work as customers than they do at home as consumers.

Online customers do not all behave the same way. For example, the assumption that banner ads would continue to outperform magazine ads and direct mail even after the novelty wore off was a bad one. Smart marketers have learned that unless these ads are targeted and connected to other marketing messages, customers won't bite. Likewise, assuming that email would become a 'beacon' into the hearts and minds of customers has fallen short of expectations. In reality, online readers are sick of email marketing. Seventy percent of experienced online readers have at least three addresses screening email. Online customers are becoming increasingly selective about the brands they trust, and what they consider relevant.

A survey of 400 online customers conducted by IMT Strategies in 2000 and again a year later highlights several aspects of customer behaviour that translate directly into marketing results. It shows that customer expectations about privacy policies, frequency, message context, personalisation, and ease of response are important to the design and execution of online marketing programs. These 'customer design points' must be the framework that influences decisions about management practices and investments today.

Important issues to start understanding and managing online customers include the following:

Context	Making campaigns and offers relevant.
Personalisation	Optimising investments in personalisation and customisation.
Frequency	Managing campaign frequency and customer overload.
Privacy	Adhering to customer privacy standards, trends, and expectations.
Permission	Building relationships through permission marketing and practices.
E-care	Meeting customer expectations for e-care and response management.
Responsiveness	Understanding the drivers of purchase and response.

Over time, as more is learned about customer buying behaviour, smart marketers will isolate campaign and program characteristics that drive response and action. Isolating the behaviour of high-value customers, business customers, or the minority of customers who prefer to buy online will be critical. For example, new online buyers get referrals when shopping online, while experienced frequent buyers prefer search engines. The ability to distinguish the differences between shoppers and buyers will be increasingly important to proper market segmentation and to the allocation and performance of online marketing budget.

The lifetime value of a customer

For most businesses, the most valuable business asset isn't on the balance sheet. It's their customer list. The hardest, most expensive sale we ever make to a customer is the first one. In that first, critical transaction we earn or lose the trust of the customer. Once we have the trust of the customer, we open the door to many more sales and to referrals. Many businesses frantically work at bringing in new businesses while they neglect developing the core of opportunity represented by their customer list. The lifetime value of a customer is the potential contribution of the customer to your business over a period of time. When you know the lifetime value of a customer, you have a benchmark for how much you should be willing to invest to acquire a customer.

Four steps for internet marketing

One of the most critical lessons about internet marketing you can learn is that your visitors don't think of themselves as part of an audience, but as an individual customer who has arrived at your front door seeking information. And that is how they want to be treated.

> The successful company will never lose sight of this fundamental fact: Whether the customer encounters your message by television, radio, print or the web, buying still first takes place in the mind. The fundamental rules of recognising and satisfying the motivations of your customers still apply.

So, how do you begin to create or analyse your web site to maximize its marketing power?

Step One

Determine why you want a web site. Do you want to provide information, enhance customer service, sell products or services, prospect for customers, build name ID and image, etc.? While a number of companies are making money by direct selling, most find that their web site is best for generating inquiries.

Step Two

Determine whom you want to reach online. You'll probably have several categories here, since the internet is now attracting a wide range of people. Don't forget to consider visitors from other countries. Can people in Scotland or Paris or Moscow use your product? Imagine that your store has ten thousand doors, and just on the other side of those doors are offices and spare bedrooms in England, Dallas, Adelaide, Berne, Iceland and every little town and big city in between. That's how close your customers are now.

Step Three

Write down all the reasons these visitors might want, need or desire your product, all the fears they may have associated with buying it, e.g. it won't work, it's poor value and all the fears they may have associated with not buying it, e.g. insurance costs too much. Remember, people don't want your product or service; they want to satisfy some motivation.

Step Four

Write down all the features of your product or service, your product or service category, your offer, your guarantee, your service, etc. which will satisfy their motivations. Only after you have this put together all this information are you ready to begin thinking about your web site. Because until you know who your targeted visitors will be, why they are looking around your virtual shopfront, and what they're looking for, you can't create a place that will be the most appealing to them. Here are a few things to remember about the minds of your internet visitors:

- They are looking for something. Most site visitors won't just be browsing. They have come to find more information about something specific, whether it is a new computer or the latest research on cancer.
- They have a lot of sites to choose from. Always remember that you are only a click away from oblivion. If they don't like what they find or how it is offered, they can be in the next merchant's store in a few seconds.
- Television viewers recognise that millions of others are watching the same program, but internet viewers don't have that mindset. They have the mindset of a caller who has rung up the shop or dropped in to look at a product. They see themselves as individuals, and want to be treated that way.
- They are jealous of their privacy. Imagine a customer comes into your real-world shop. Would an assistant approach them with a clipboard and ask for their name, address, and favourite colour? Of course not. Online visitors will reluctantly give you some information about themselves, but only if there is something in it for them, e.g. a discount. Treat them with consideration and courtesy, just like they were in your shop.
- They are worried about giving out their credit card numbers. This is slowly changing, but it is still overwhelmingly the biggest barrier to e-commerce today. They want to know that you have a secure payment system to protect them, and an alternate way to buy if they're still nervous.
- They are jealous of their time. They don't want to wait. The relatively small bandwidth now carrying internet messages creates slow downloads, especially if there are large graphic files. While the full frame colour shot of your virtual shopfront is taking twenty seconds to appear on their monitor, they are getting more impatient. No one likes waiting in line, even on the internet.
- They are not expert navigators. Imagine looking for a book in a massive library, but with no librarians. That's what it is like for many people who try to find information online. It is easy for them to get frustrated and angry when your site doesn't take them by the hand and lead them to the right place.

- They may like to look at visually exciting sites, but that isn't what makes most of them come back. People bookmark a site because it provides what they want, and makes it easy to get.

Coca-Cola and Procter & Gamble are just two of the industry giants that are using the web in a big way. And many leading dot.com e-tailers, including Amazon.com, eBay and eToys, view the web as a primary way of finding and attracting customers. According to a report from Simba Information Inc., a US based market intelligence and forecasting firm, spending for online advertising will hit $7.1 billion during 2002, up from $2.1 billion in 1998. Jupiter Media Metrix Inc., a market intelligence company based in New York City, predicts that online advertising will soon become the fourth leading advertising medium, trailing only television, radio and newspapers.

Your online marketing maintenance plan

Here's an example of an integrated e-marketing program roadmap with actions at each stage:

Daily marketing tasks
- Follow up all leads (and answer your email)

Weekly marketing tasks
- Evaluate your daily tracking reports
- Review your web page stats
- Utilise free marketing resources
- Post a communication to a bulletin board.
- Post an ad to opt-in e-groups
- Post an ad to a discussion group
- Update your 'My Affiliate Records'
- Initiate a Pay Per Click Program
- Add a page to your website.

Monthly marketing tasks
- Submit any new web pages to at least 5 new search engines. As soon as you're in the major engines such as Excite, go for the next level of engines like MetaCrawler.
- Find one new ezine to advertise in.
- Submit an article to a list of targeted ezine publishers.

- Review your autoresponder setup
- E-mail your current database

Quarterly marketing tasks
- Set up on completely automated marketing tool.
- Sign on one joint venture.

Pick one or two things you can do every day to promote your website and work them into your schedule. These should be little things that won't take too long, like soliciting a link from a new website and/or participating in a newsgroup or discussion list. Decide how often it is reasonable for you to try a new method. Once a month may be good timing, but if you're very busy, it may be more reasonable to go for once every three months. Put it into your schedule. Test every new method you try. Ask people how they are finding your website, or include tracking codes on your URL (www.domain.com/?code) or use special pages to keep track of how many people are attracted to your website through each advertisement. If you know what isn't working, you can focus your time and money on what does. Decide what you consider an advertising success.

The most important thing is how many people were attracted to your website compared to how much time and money you spent. To decide how many visitors is really enough, you may need to determine how much money a visitor is really worth. How often do visitors buy your products or services? How much money do you get for advertisements on your website per visitor? Do your visitors return often? Figure in the average number of return visits, if you can. The lifetime value of each visitor is what counts here. Once you know how much each visitor is worth to you, check to make sure your advertising efforts are not costing more in your time and money than you are making through the visitors they attract.

Remember to schedule in time to continue and improve campaigns, which have worked. Once a week, work on current campaigns, write a new ad, or find a new place to buy or exchange ads (using a method which has worked in the past). Where should you place your ads? Who do you want to visit your website? Where do they hang out on the internet? What about off-line? Find out where you can reach your target audience, and put it in your marketing plan. Keep on marketing track, and you will get better profits in the long run.

2

Brand Marketing

CLICK-ONS

Branding

E-Male?

Benchmarking

Brand crisis management

360-degree branding

9 ways to brand your site

A brand health check

Branding

When passing through Charles De Gaulle airport in Paris, you notice the billboards – their messages change. Not just the simple capacity to switch between three different displays as most outdoor billboards around the world are able to do. These billboards exhibit unlimited change and display whatever message is required at any particular second. How is this possible? The billboards are actually digital TV screens that link directly to the outdoor-display company's database.

Cross the Channel to London where people are busier typing text messages into their mobile phones than they are using the phones for conversation.

Soon, when our internet connections are no longer dependent on dial-up modems but are always on, 24 hours a day, 7 days a week, we'll notice that our web use will change dramatically. Instant commercial messages and emails will acquire new significance: for example, they might offer 50 percent discounts for customers who respond within five minutes of receiving a promotional message.

Those three instances are realities, or very close to being realities and the scenario they paint for marketers include an interesting challenge, which is summarised by the term 'instant branding.'

Ten years ago, you had to plan a TV campaign at least a year ahead. You had to book it at least three months ahead, and you had to start production at least four months prior to airing. That lead-time has evaporated – the months of preparation have now been reduced to hours.

Take these three imaginary scenarios:

❑ Imagine that Shell Oil faces an environmental controversy of some sort. Instant branding would allow the company's marketers to communicate a clever message via all instant media channels within hours, circumventing the growth of any negative publicity in the marketplace and restoring the desired equilibrium to public perception.

❑ Imagine that your competitor decides to drop its product prices by 5 percent. Instant branding would mean that you could respond appropriately with all due expediencies, using instant media channels.

❑ Imagine that the temperature hits 90 degrees Fahrenheit. Coke's marketing machine might be triggered into action, sending instant commercial messages that promote a 'heat wave' sales drive.

Instant branding is a challenging tool; it deteriorates marketing plans that depend on one and two-year time frames. Instant branding both puts into question and calls on the advertising business's ability to manage brands cleverly, spontaneously, and within a flexible strategy.

Some 70 years ago, Coca-Cola gave its designer a special brief: Design a bottle that no matter how smashed could always be recognised among all the thousands of glass shards on the street. Today, we can still recognise the distinctive Coke bottle. Imagine that we performed the same test on your website. Imagine we smashed it by searching through every page and deleting the brand and any references to it – and then asked the consumer to visit the site without knowing what its brand was. Do you think your site would pass the Coke test? This is what true branding is. Integrated, consistent elements that in isolation are signifiers of a brand but together create the full brand identity. A logo can be nice because it states identity. But the reality is that consumers don't usually sit and watch your logo on your site. Customers visit for information or service. They read text, look at pictures, fill out forms, ask questions, and try some of the interactivity the site offers. All these elements should, by principle, communicate branded experiences that together establish a full picture of your brand.

An Australian bank recently conducted a test that showed the long waiting time on the bank's site was parallel, in the customers' estimation, to tedious queuing in the real-world bank. The same study showed that spelling errors on the site also weakened the brand's credibility. Customers felt that they couldn't trust a bank that wasn't professional enough to identify and eliminate spelling errors.

The customer's experience of your site is enhanced or devalued by everyone of its elements, including the emails you send. Your wording, tone of voice, and the message's objective all reflect your brand's position. And your handling of these elements should be taken just as seriously as the production of an advertisement.

A well known, high-class car company used John Cleese to promote its brand on television and the internet. The promotion was a major success; consumers loved Cleese on the site. However, a problem arose. Once the campaign ended, it was discovered that brand awareness hadn't changed a single percent. And sales even decreased. The John Cleese element did not express the brand's core values. Even though TV viewers and site visitors loved his comedic character, they had difficulty associating him with the brand he was representing. Additionally, Cleese was perceived as such a strong brand himself that his persona blocked the car brand's exposure, leaving it the loser in the campaign.

Brand building on the internet means much more than getting your logo right. Because we can't satisfy our senses of smell, taste, and touch on the net, we compensate by employing 'brand translation.' We translate visual and aural impressions to gain a virtual sense of a product or promise. Every element on a web site including colour, copy, font, image, and sound, builds your brand and leaves impressions in consumers' minds. Impressions that are formed by their liking of the brand, their trust in it, and their potential reliance on it. Your brand needs to work extra hard to compensate for the experiential gaps of sensory deprivation, anonymity and isolation.

According to a recent Morgan Stanley (**www.morganstanley.com**) study, banner ads were more effective at generating brand interest than ads on TV or in newspapers or magazines. Consumers show a 27 percent greater ability to recall a brand after seeing an ad online. The challenge still remains: how to 'sell' branding online to implement and execute a successful campaign. How can we measure return on investment (ROI)? In a Jupiter (**www.jmm.com**) survey, only 15 percent of marketers said that they are conducting formal online branding measurement. Analysts suggest that marketers can measure branding value by correlating behavioural data (including user click-streams, repeated surfing patterns, and aggregate user behaviour) with the flights of specific ads. Here are eight things to bear in mind with regard to branding online:

1. The use of multiple ad units only enhances a media buy.
2. Because your brand is strong offline, don't assume it will be so online.
3. Online advertising raises brand awareness. Online and offline media strategies, creative messaging, and key metrics must align to achieve success.
4. Third-party ad serving and site activity reports cannot be standalone.
5. Log file analysis, data from other online initiatives e.g. affiliate marketing, search engine optimisation, etc. should be married with ad activity data and key findings.
6. Evaluating multiple metrics yields a higher ROI.

AdKnowledge (**www.adknowledge.com**) found that 32 percent of a site's conversions come from users who viewed an ad and did not click on it. Multiple exposures to an ad will increase brand awareness. Initiate user studies and traffic reports. As you are in the midst of planning, think about campaign-tracking goals. You may want to consider the following:

- Do the ads complement and integrate with offline advertising messages?
- Do the ads help build key perceptions of the brand?
- Do the ads enhance the brand's relationship with the customer?
- Do the ads impact the consumer's next opportunity to buy?

What makes a good online brand name?

It is not the name that matters, but what it represents. That is why online communities such as Yahoo!, America Online and eBay are the best examples of online brand success stories so far. It is clear that brand building, however important, cannot be achieved all at once, whether from a domain name purchase, or from all-out media blitzes. The brand name, and goodwill it represents, may be the most valuable asset held by some e-businesses.

> A study by the Centre for Research in Brand Marketing at the University of Birmingham found that tangible assets make up only one-quarter of the full value of the average business. The other three-fourths is largely attributed to the value of that company's brand identity.

The smartest e-commerce firms may be those that find a way to latch onto existing brand names in the brick-and-mortar world. By co-branding with traditional merchants, virtual retailers without brand names can gain a stake in the market, gain credibility and trust and drive traffic and they can do it fairly quickly and inexpensively.

For brand awareness experts, the good news is that the day when a company would spend millions of pounds on a domain name, such as Business.com appears to be over. If anything, some dot.coms are going to the opposite extreme. Companies such as Internet.com decided to jettison the 'dot-com' part of their names in an apparent attempt to distance themselves from the stigma of the dot-com shakeout. Having the phrase 'dot-com' attached to a brand name might make a transition to a brick-and-mortar presence trickier, observers say. Names like Yahoo! and Amazon, for example, can go anywhere, while Furniture.com does not travel quite as well. The more open-ended the name, the greater the opportunity to expand into new markets. In the end, however, one overriding rule has emerged. When it comes to online branding, the name does not make the company – the company makes the name.

Your domain name

Turn your web site name into a branding tool by using your company or product name, such as **www.easypccomputer.com**. If possible, don't use numbers, underline marks, meaningless words or abbreviations few people will understand.

E-Male?

The internet is no longer mostly for, or by, boys. Women, especially those between the ages of 18 and 34, are becoming a significant force in adopting new technologies and engaging in sophisticated internet use, according to a poll of 2,000 Canadian internet users. A POLLARA (**www.pollara.ca**) survey found that more than 40 percent of the most frequent and sophisticated internet users are women. That's up from the 30 percent claimed by the previous year's study.

Most web sites clearly reflect a lack of an appreciation of the female user's psyche and approach to inquiry and tasks. By now the internet is part of mainstream communication media. So the flexibility, accessibility, and straightforwardness of traditional communication channels should be forming part of the internet's operational repertoire as well.

Most web sites, if not nearly all of them, look like index pages from the Stock Exchange. They use stock photos, often of people shaking hands or grasping something equally unoriginal, such as cell phones. The stock subjects are all clad in stereotypical colours. Presentation is not a superficial issue. It's a *vital part* of a site's message, and it's an invitation to the user to navigate her way toward a brand's objectives. If you're a woman currently reading this book, it's likely to have been some time since you encountered a web site that elicited a response from you such as: 'What a useful and intriguing web site. Great message, logical navigation, memorable personality. I'll certainly return to the site.' On the other hand, when did you last visit a site and leave as quickly as possible, weighed down with an impression such as this: 'What an incredibly boring and unrewarding site. What were they trying to tell me/sell/achieve?'

One of the reasons site design has been so apparently uninformed by the driving need to gain and hold human interest is that most site builders have to date been men. In fact, an Australian survey shows that men have designed 85 percent of web sites. But the female portion of the world's technology and programming population is growing rapidly. The result is likely to be navigation and style characteristics that better reflect an appreciation of human interaction and a broader understanding of communication needs. The real world of men, women, and children – the elderly and the young, the informed specialists and the generalists – will at last be reflected in cyberspace.

Benchmarking

How good is your brand? When is your brand good enough? When do you decide that your brand has reached the highest possible level? Benchmarking provides a way to figure out how good your brand can possibly be.

Take a brand like Disney World and analyse how benchmarking could be used to ascertain the quality of the consumer experience. The total Disney World experience is made up of lots of small experiences that compose the full brand picture.

1   First comes the decision about where to go. For this, a brand needs to have stamped its awareness into the consumer's mind.

    NOTE: In terms of awareness, Pepsi and McDonald's are good examples. Awareness comes with an impression of an overriding reputation. What will your brand's dominant reputation be for? Quality, like Hewlett-Packard? Convenience? Family-friendliness?

2   Second, travelling to the park. Easy access will be the aim.

    NOTE: Hertz airport kiosks spring to mind as offering easy access: They're conveniently located and easy to find. McDonald's also provides a well-beaten and easy-to-follow path to its doors.

3   Third, entering the park.

    NOTE: Some of the world's leading airports, like Hong Kong's, Copenhagen's, and Malaysia's, would probably offer examples of a pleasant, crowd-pleasing, well-controlled entry.

4   Fourth, the greeting.

    NOTE: Friendly and casual greetings, inspired by a Club-Med type personalities might be the comparative measure. Purchasing the ticket may be inspired by Hertz procedure.

Being a top brand isn't about being the best in one category. It's about being the best in all the details. Together, these create the full brand reputation.

Brand crisis management

Recently, Yahoo.com managed to get its name mentioned in most media around the world. But this time, it wasn't positive news that brought public attention to the Yahoo! brand. The stimulus was from Yahoo! in France where its online auction site included Nazi paraphernalia – Nazi medals, clothing, ephemera, and other artefacts – all available to the highest bidder. The crisis was over the French government's ban on racist representation in all media. The French authorities saw Yahoo!'s auction listings as an infringement of its jurisdictional authority. This was not a predictable crisis, even for the most experienced brand experts. But it happened to ensnare the well-respected Yahoo! brand, which had to suddenly deal with a problem fraught with negative associations.

Brand crisis-management programs predict possibilities and prepare for hypothetical eventualities. Plans are developed and tested to minimise the ill effects of crises when they occur. Crises will affect online brands, too. Consumers are as sceptical about online commerce as they are about offline commerce. So, you'll have to think through every possible crisis; create detailed action plans to accompany each hypothetical scenario; and analyse management responsibilities of everyone who's part of your business. And do it now. Crises don't disappear. But they can be managed with common sense.

360-degree branding

Over the past years, thousands of companies have been unable to establish a good reputation among their consumer audience because these companies failed to achieve synergy between their strategic intentions and the real outcomes the market perceived.

> During 1999, Nike diluted its brand dramatically. The 'Just Do It' ethos became a nightmare tagline when it became global knowledge that Nike exploited labour in Third World countries. 'Just Do It' was translated into counter-campaign T-shirts bearing the slogan 'Just Don't Do It.' Thus the philosophy and marketing drive that Nike had spent years creating came crashing down.

This fatality has to do with 180-degree branding. Quick branding doesn't exist. This is the type of dilemma facing most dot.com sites. In the split second that it takes to make a purchase from the site, or worse, during the longer time you might spend contacting it with requests for information or to return products, it is then that the shit hits the fan. So far, dot.com branding has covered the first 10 degrees. What about the other 350?

A recent study conducted by Bang & Olufsen (**www.bang-olufsen.com**), the high-quality stereo-equipment manufacturer, shows that the future of branding doesn't lie in imaging, the product itself, or the ads. It's the whole brand story that counts.

The risk of everything falling apart is huge, and this might be the reason why up to 25 percent of users who fail to use an online site satisfactorily decide never to return to the site again (Forrester Research: **www.forrester.com**). Sites like this kill their brands, even before birth. Three-hundred-and-sixty-degree branding is about creating a solid brand philosophy.

Nine ways to brand your website

☑ If five hundred people visit your website, maybe one of them will email you. Those people are your best contacts! Answer their email warmly and personally, and not only will they return, but they'll bring their friends. You may get spam, but those messages are easy to weed out.

☑ If your visitors remember your name, they'll come back when they need the information, products or services offered on your website. Compel people to remember, and your website will blossom.

☑ Give your visitors a reason to return to your website often by offering valuable content updated frequently.

☑ If possible, remind them to come back with a newsletter or announcement list.

☑ Make sure your articles and information are on the same topic. If you are interested in writing articles on other topics, consider publishing them elsewhere (email magazines and newsletters may be easier to break into, but also consider print publications) or buying separate domain names for each topic.

☑ All the text on your website should have the same tone. Make everything sound uniquely you. The more unique and personal your text reads, the more people will like and remember your website.

☑ Remember to give your visitors a way to contact a real person at your website. The more personal attention they get, the more they will remember you and your website or business.

☑ Compel visitors to remember your website with a unique and consistent design (including colour scheme), a distinctive logo, a consistent navigational system, and contact information on every page.

☑ Let your visitors know who you are when they're on your website. Offer a link to information about yourself and your organisation. A history or philosophy and a personal biography can increase the intimacy of your website.

A Brand Health Check

Tone of voice

The tone of voice your brand adopts reflects two things: your ability to convey your brand's spirit and personality in written and verbal communication; and your ability to pitch your communication style appropriately for your audience. Too much information can complicate the language, destroying its ability to define the brand and defusing its core message. Pick five of your site's pages at random. Now ask a couple of independent people to read them. Their task will be to tell you whether the five pages manage, individually, to target their consumer needs and whether they believe the five pages are consistent with each other.

Match consumer expectations

What do your users expect from your site when they visit? Do they expect to gain more knowledge? To be able to purchase your product at a discount? To gain access to a wider range of products or services or certain information? To be entertained? You might know what you would expect from the site, but your expectations may be different from your audience's. Have you investigated what your consumer actually wants from your site, and, if you have, was your site at least 75 percent on point in meeting those expectations?

Consistency

Consistency is especially important when it comes to navigation. You should ensure that your brand's core message is reflected consistently in your site's navigation, that consumers can rely on your communications consistency to navigate their way from page to page, from your real-world shop to your site, from your mobile to your site, from your catalogue to your site, and so on. In short, ensure that your consumer, at any point on your brand's communications continuum, knows without any doubt where to go and why to go there. Consistency ensures synergy between the brand's messages across all media channels. How consistent is your brand's web site message (its voice and utterances) with the message it promotes in the shops? How consistent is your television message with its radio exposure? With its coverage in catalogues? Can you claim that at least 50 percent of the message (tone and content) is consistent across media channels?

Give them a reason to return Amazon.com expects its customers to stay with it for at least 10 years. What is your expectation of your consumer lifespan? Are you delivering enough to re-attract your visitors time after time? Are you offering enough exceptional offers? Enough news? Enough exclusive data? Yes, it's important to attract new customers. But it's even more important to retain them, especially since retention costs about one-tenth of acquisition.

Keep your brand's promise If you promise to deliver within 24 hours, deliver within 23 hours. If you promise to accept product returns without any questions asked, return the money without asking a single question. If you promise to update your news section every day, update it every day. If you promise to answer any email inquiries within 24 hours, do it in 20 hours.

Surprise customers positively Imagine you were able to predict everything you saw on television today or everything you read in the paper. Wouldn't that be boring? So after visiting your site once, would someone be able to predict what it would offer them on their next visit? Or would they be positively surprised not only during their first visit but also on each subsequent visit? Surprising your customers in a positive way builds your brand by creating excitement and loyalty. Would you be able to surprise 50 percent of your audience every time they visit your site?

Key message Is your core message clear to your web site's audience? What three key messages should your site's visitors take away with them after having spent 10 minutes on your site?

Listening, learning, and reacting Brands that are able to listen to consumer information, learn from the data, and react with the consumer intelligently will be winners. Assess how good you, as the brand-builder, are at listening to your consumers, capturing relevant information about them, learning from the data by mining the tons of information you gather and analysing it – and by reflecting your findings in intelligent one-to-one dialogue with the consumer.

Remove the logo Remove all your logos from your site, remove all brand names, and then ask the consumer to visit your site and guess to which brand it belongs. If 70 percent of your visitors mention your brand, your web site is on track. It means that you have managed to involve every communications element in your brand message, that you've translated every design detail, text inclusion, colour scheme, and so on as meaningful contributors to your brand's consistent message. In theory, your logo should no longer be necessary to identify the brand.

Studies promote web ad branding power

Four new research studies were presented that give new weight to the argument that online ads are effective branding tools. In a joint presentation, the Interactive Advertising Bureau and member companies DoubleClick and MSN, unveiled their individual studies on the effectiveness of branding on the internet in New York City. Separately, CNET Networks released information from a study done with Millward Brown IntelliQuest. Results from each of the four studies support the assertion that web ads brand. For example, the IAB study conducted by Dynamic Logic found that the new larger ad units are 25 percent more effective in lifting key brand metrics such as brand awareness and message association – even at one exposure. The research also shows that additional exposures significantly increase persuasion metrics such as purchase intent. The research was based on 8,750 respondents, four advertisers and 12 creative units.

The goal of DoubleClick's online marketing effectiveness study was to determine the impact of various online marketing tactics on traditional brand marketing goals. Across each online marketing unit tested, traditional brand measures including aided brand awareness, aided advertising awareness, ad attribute recall and ad recall increased considerably. Aggregated results for three brands across each online marketing tactic tested, showed an 85 percent increase in aided advertising awareness. Banner ads increased brand measures 56 percent and large rectangles 86 percent, while interstitial ads increased brand measures 194 percent.

Also working with Dynamic Logic, MSN tested two campaigns with different creative formats and sizes for two advertisers, uBid and ShareBuilder. The study found that the Skyscraper creative size worked best, lifting brand awareness by 16 percent, four times the average lift among all campaigns Dynamic Logic has tested. The study also found that interactive, DHTML units lifted awareness by 13 percent, greatly outperforming both the Dynamic Logic average and double the performance of the non-interactive creative in the campaigns.

Meanwhile, CNET's study, performed by Millward Brown IntelliQuest, was an attempt to determine the effectiveness of its new rich media interactive advertising units, also known as Messaging Plus Units. According to the Millward Brown IntelliQuest research, Messaging Plus Units prove to have significant 'stopping power,' and also enhance aided and unaided brand recall as well as positively impact brand purchase consideration after a single exposure. Forty-two percent of respondents remembered seeing the MPU ad after viewing it only once. Ad brand recognition increased 30 percent over the control group, and users remembered not only seeing the ad, but also associated the ad with its respective brand.

3

Marketing at the Website Design Stage

CLICK-ONS

Wireframing

Starting to design your website

YOURNAME.COM

Creating content

The best websites

Writing for the internet

Making the most of keywords

13 questions for website designers

Wireframing

Many people confuse storyboarding with wireframing, or they believe that because they are storyboarding they have already done a wireframe. Wireframing involves making a skeleton of your web site that focuses only on what you want the site to DO in response to each user click, not on how that gets done:

- Wireframing is about the concept of what the site needs to do. It has nothing to do with the developer's, programmer's, or designer's concepts of how to get it done.

- A wireframe is an enhanced flowchart without graphical images that demonstrates every click-through possibility on your site. Wireframing is about defining the entry points to, and exit points from, each page. It answers questions such as 'What actions can be taken here?' and 'What is the user's state of experience as she enters this page and when she leaves it?' It focuses on the click-through sequence and user-experience flow of the site.

- A proper wireframe does not have any design, copywriting, programming, or other components; those, at this first stage, serve only to distract you from clarifying exactly what your site must do, and must not do, at every point in your visitor's click-through journey.

Although wireframing may have started as a software development tool, it has a much broader application. It allows you to define the motivation behind every page and the function of each page, and it allows you to determine whether a page really needs to be there. Wireframing also allows you to make sure that each page has a clear call to action that motivates the visitor to go forward.

Wireframing helps you to conceptualise what your site needs to do and how the customer experience should be built. With the HTML wireframe approach, you are actually interacting with a functioning model of your web site almost from the beginning and long before a single question of design or copy or even colour gets addressed. You can click on links and see where they go. You can begin to feel what it will be like to use your site rather than just see it. Wireframing is all about the execution and process of the site and has nothing to do with innovations of technology or design.

Starting to design your website

If your site can't lead your customers successfully through the key processes of shopping and buying, your business is going to wind up as a dot.bomb. Before you program a single page, do the following:

- Spend the time necessary to understand the elements involved in creating an interactive sales machine.
- Thoroughly consider your web site from your visitor's point of view.
- Wireframe the user experience.
- Create your storyboard.

The storyboard looks a lot like a flow chart, with paper pages representing each individual web page. Each sheet describes the web page and contains a summary of its content, layout, elements, and objectives. The main objectives of every page are to motivate your customers to engage them, to make it simple for them to take the desired action and, ultimately, to satisfy them after they take the action. The sheets representing web pages then can be arranged in the logical order of the buying process, with arrows between the pages. These arrows will become the links you provide to help your customers navigate through your site, find what they want quickly, and buy it easily. There should be various arrow paths representing differing outcomes, based on how your customers might move through the site. Some of the arrow paths may even be circular, since the buying process is a system of feedback loops.

Studies consistently prove shoppers find ease of process far more pleasing than glitz and gloss. Never forget: the ultimate purpose of your site is not to dazzle, but to sell.

Make sure that each and every element in your storyboard addresses these critical questions:

? What do I want my visitors to know here?
? What do I want my visitors to do at this point?
? What do I want my visitors to feel right now?
? Where do I want my visitors to go next?
? How do I make it easy for them to do that?
? How do I 'reinforce' them after they've done it?

Consider every conceivable option. Sometimes customers miss the home page and arrive mid-site. Will they know where they are, where they can go, what they are supposed to do? That's what your final storyboard is for: designing the site to allow customers to enter your site anywhere, know where they are, and quickly understand how they can get to where they want to be.

**GET YOURSELF A PROFITABLE DOT.COM
NOT A MONEY-LOSING DOT.BOMB**

Keep graphics to a minimum, and be sure every graphic is important to the visitor. One good technique is to create a series of small photos (thumbnails) on the page, each of which the visitor can click to see a full screen version. Animated visuals can also take time to download – remember that most visitors are coming onto your site for information, not entertainment.

Navigation tips

There are numerous navigation schemes. Hierarchical, global, supplemental, and embedded links are the most common. Hierarchical navigation helps people keep track of how deep into the site they are. For example, global navigation schemes, such as tabs, help direct the customer to what type of products and services are available. Supplemental or local navigation allows users to get to related information within a category rather than between categories, e.g. HR books: employment law, training, recruitment. This is particularly helpful when your visitor has landed on your site via a search engine but hasn't landed on the right page. The navigation scheme important to actually closing sales is the embedded-links scheme. Within the body of your copy, you simply place links to the places you want prospects to go next. If embedded links are done well, they will engage your users effectively as they browse within the 'active window' of your site. The active window is the main area of your page, underneath or to the side of your main navigation. It is where you place your body text, display your products, and present your offer. It is also where you want to keep your visitors' eyes focused. If you properly engage them in this area by providing the right choices to click on, you persuade them to follow the path you want them to take. This is also why it is very important to keep a consistent look and feel around the active window.

Have simple and consistent navigation. Your average prospect will view two to three pages before leaving; so, at best, you're two clicks away from being dead in the water unless you help them get where they want to go quickly. Never leave your prospect stranded anywhere on your site. Imagine you're lost in the middle of a huge department store with no signs. Where's kitchenware? Where's do I pay? Where's the loo? So, on your site, provide clear navigation from anywhere to anywhere, and do it on every page and keep all your navigation links within your page. Unless you want to encourage your customers to leave, don't direct them to the Back button on the browser.

> Dr. Ralph Wilson, publisher of 'Web Marketing Today' (**www.wilsonweb.com**), writes, 'Inadequate navigation design is probably the main failing of business websites.' Assuming some visitors have overcome the first hurdle of finding out that your site exists, you've then got to convince them you have what they want. To do that, you must help them find the exact information they need, quickly and easily. That's the role of your navigation tools.

Can visitors immediately see how to navigate your web site? Many sites have dozens of pages. Your visitors want to get to the exact page they need quickly, which means *within two or three clicks*. If your navigation tools are unclear, your visitors will be frustrated. It is critical that you give visitors a menu of options on the homepage. The best way to make the menu helpful is to select clear, specific terms for each category of information. Visitors would much rather look down a long list of options if it will get them where they want to go. If you have over thirty or forty different categories of information within several section titles, consider putting them in a drop-down menu, which appears when a visitor selects a section name.

A navigation menu on the left side of the page is fast becoming the design standard. It shows visitors all the navigation options you offer. It's a good idea to provide this basic navigation tool on every page. If you have a large web site with many topics, consider providing a 'search' option that will lead visitors right to the information they want.

The three standard links for any site:

1   Allows the visitor to send you an e-mail.

2   Shows the visitor answers to some Frequently Asked Questions (FAQs).

3   Provides Help in navigating the site, filling out forms, definitions, accomplishing what they came to do and providing helpful ideas for any possible confusing situation.

One-to-one-marketing

One-to-one marketing is rapidly becoming the standard by which all marketing is measured. Underneath the surface of internet one-to-one marketing is internet personalisation. Although the original definition of personalisation in marketing meant using a person's name or other personal information in a communication, today it has taken on a much broader meaning. Personalisation often crosses lines with customisation, which is the packaging of information in a customised way.

An example of highly personalised customer service is the way Amazon.com advises its customers on purchasing. Amazon makes 'instant recommendations,' suggesting items that the customer might be interested in based on previous purchases, and offers ideas for complementary items. For example, if you select a computer printer, Amazon will recommend cartridges and printer cables to go along with it. Amazon also provides '1-Click ordering,' which customises the ordering process so returning customers don't have to re-enter basic data already on file.

The presence of 'my' pages at a growing number of sites (at portals and search engines in particular), is evidence of the growth of personalisation. 'My' pages give users individual power to customise home pages and other web pages to meet their specific needs. These pages typically use personalisation engines and tools that provide users with choices, usually in the form of check boxes, from which to select personalisation criteria. By answering a few simple questions, the user instructs the web site to 'learn' his or her preferences, so a personalised page appears the next time.

> Personalisation isn't only for web sites. More and more, email programs are incorporating sophisticated use of personalisation, not just a name within the email copy but personal information throughout the email strategy. Programmed email is used so that an individual receives the right email at the right time.

In the context of building customer relationships, there does appear to be strong evidence that customising and personalising the experience leads to greater customer loyalty and higher customer retention rates. According to eMarketer, a recent study reported that 63 percent of US consumers are more likely to register at a web site that accommodates content customisation and offers personalisation features.

The latest research found that the average person would leave a site which doesn't download within EIGHT SECONDS.

YOURNAME.COM

According to some sources, roughly 26 million domain names (almost half of which are .com domains) have been registered, and new ones are being taken at a 60,000-per-day clip. Now that the initial panic buy has subsided, many people who grabbed domains because 'they were there' are letting their registrations lapse, and some words have never been taken.

Make the name a single word or combination of a couple of words

Amazon.com, Yahoo!, eBay and Google are all prime examples of this principle. If the list of words gets too long, you may have trouble getting something memorable. For example **thebestkitchenssinceslicedbread.com** is a bit too long to easily roll off the tongue. Blue Mountain Arts are exceptions to this rule, but even so Blue Mountain has changed its URL to **bluemountain.com**.

The new maximum length for domain names is 67 characters, including the .com portion

Use easy-to-spell words

A URL such as **miscellanymemoirs.com** is just begging for trouble. If you cannot use plain English words, made-up words with English, Latin, or Greek roots, at least make aural and visual sense to most internet users, e.g. Intel. Something like **reykjaviklive.com** would be a bit tricky to type in after one hearing on the radio.

Non-alphabet characters should be used with care

You cannot register a domain name with any characters other than the 26 standard English alphabet letters, numerals 0-9, and the hyphen (-). Still, enough confusion can arise from the use of these. Take, for example, the domain name **4-web-guide.com**. If a friend told you about the site and said 'four web guide dot com,' what would you type in? Probably 'forwebguide.com' or 'fourwebguide.com.' Unless you've seen the name in print, you're not likely to pick up on the numeral '4' and the hyphens.

Abbreviations carry their own hidden dangers

One problem with abbreviations is that you're never sure how to use them, since in everyday speech we tend to unabbreviate them. This is a tricky ploy for a web site, unless you're IBM or as clever as Procter & Gamble, which uses both **pg.com** and **pandg.com**.

Creating content

Part of your web strategy and design planning requires that you think through the type of content that would be most appropriate, who your audience is, and how you'll create that content and keep it fresh and interesting. Content is the primary reason that people visit your site. You're writing content to attract and keep visitors on your site (a concept known as 'stickiness'), to get them to return again and again, and to sell your products or services. Your content can generate page views; the more page views your site serves up and the more traffic it generates, the more money you can charge advertisers to place banner ads on your site.

Examples of the types of content you could include are: contact information, company history, profiles of key people, frequently asked questions, press releases, customer testimonials, product or service features and articles about your products or services in action, and helpful tips. Providing information via articles could invite inquiries from people interested in hiring your services. The same can be true for a product that requires considerable aftermarket servicing. You can use your web site to build trust in your products and expertise.

> Within the context of your overall budget, come up with a range of how much you want to spend to put content on your site, and then to maintain it and keep it current. It usually costs more to commission content than it does to refresh it or check it periodically for accuracy. Don't forget to consider the costs of taking people away from their primary responsibilities to create content.

You could generate your own text and graphical content by drawing on your existing in-house talent or you could recruit outside content creators. Creating your own content gives you a greater level of control over the information that is featured on your site. You can also acquire both text and graphical content from outside sources through syndicated companies that share their content. Obviously this content will likely have a broad appeal, and if your company fills a niche market, you may not find content that is appropriate.

If you post your original content and forget about it, your visitors will be able to tell. You need to keep refreshing your features to make sure your site is up to date and keep the interest of your customers. The only way you'll know whether your site is meeting your customers' needs and how it might need to be changed is to keep monitoring it after it is built. You can use a number of methods to make sure your content is right for your audience. Log analysis tools to track traffic patterns on your site, keyword tracking, and surveying your customers can all help you make sure that you don't waste your resources on content that no one is reading or that turns your customers away.

Make clear, strong text available right away. That will also keep visitors interested while graphics load. Use graphics only if they help prospects understand what they are looking for or if they convey information that can't be conveyed effectively through text. And keep graphics as simple as possible so they load quickly.

Any content should be based on the motivations of your potential on-line customers. Each page should be focused on some part of the selling process, such as image-building, good will, information, assurances and guarantees, closing, etc.

Looking at your content from a global perspective, one of the first decisions will be whether to have an English-only site, or offer information (all or partial) in certain other languages. Forrester Research found people are three times more likely to make a purchase when the web site is in their native language.

If you decide to offer at least key information in multiple languages, be very careful about using any automatic translation software. It is often insulting, or incomprehensible to your targeted customers. If you think you might have a market in France, for instance, pay someone who has lived there to do a high quality translation or look under Translators in the Yellow Pages, or talk to a language department faculty member at a local college or University.

When you're thinking about who will use the content of your web site, don't forget your partners, suppliers, and even other divisions, if your company is that big. Research by the Meta Group found that only half of the companies surveyed did e-commerce with their suppliers, and only 43% used it with their business partners. Many observers think business will see its next great cost-savings in these areas as supply chains are integrated into the internet.

The content of your home page is critical. When most visitors enter your site, they have certain motivations to satisfy. The content of your home page should stimulate those motivations, promise that you can satisfy them, and make visitors want to know more. For example, if you sell kitchen units, your home page might show people admiring a fantastic kitchen. People don't buy kitchen units only to have somewhere to put the baked beans. They buy it for the pleasure of looking at it, hearing the compliments of others, feeling pride in their decorating skills, and so on. By showing people in the picture doing some of those things, you stimulate those motivations, and promise your kitchen units will satisfy them.

Consider all the reasons visitors might want to find your site. Under each reason, list the important questions they might have when they visit your site. That is the information you'll need to provide on your web site. Take some time with this, ask some current customers, and look at it from the visitor's viewpoint. Add any other information you want them to know, such as discounts, promotions, special services, etc. Now you have what you need to begin writing the text for your web site. In nearly every situation, text, not graphics, will play a larger role in making your site successful. Next, put all these specific topics into categories e.g. price list.

If you find you have many categories, group them into some sections with titles like About Our Company. Make sure that the section and category names you pick will help visitors quickly get to the information that answers their questions. Categories answering the most frequent questions should be at the top of the list. This list should appear on the first page of your web site.

Making it interactive

Visitors want to be treated as individuals on your site. Some sites even greet returning visitors by name if they've registered before. One way to individualise your site is by making it interactive. Let your visitors interact with the database of information you have available to develop answers to their specific questions. For example, if our kitchen unit shoppers want to know how different units look together, you could offer a 'point and click' option that would put the pictures of any kitchen unit next to each other in any arrangement on the screen. Put yourself in your customer's place and ask, 'What are all the things I would like to do online at this site?' Then provide as many of those services as you can. Here are some other types of content, which will make your site more attractive to visitors:

● Offer links to other web sites with related information. You can set it up so visitors clicking on a link will see it as a window within your site –

give them information, but don't let them leave! Information-rich sites are generally the most highly rated.

- Offer freebies, e.g. discounts, coupons, BOGOFs (buy one, get one free) two-for-ones, free booklets (use an autoresponder to send them by e-mail), samples, or anything else free.

    NOTE: A story in the Wall Street Journal reported that New York stores attracted huge crowds of shoppers by advertising a 'tax free' day on merchandise. No taxes saved shoppers about 9%. 'But when we run a 10% off sale,' said a store marketing exec, 'no one cares. People just like to avoid paying taxes.'

- Provide visitors with facts that will give them confidence in your message, such as the background of your company, testimonials from satisfied customers, well-known companies you've served or been associated with, and other ways they can reach you, like your address, phone, and fax.

- Give them an e-mail link so they can easily ask you questions. Be sure to respond quickly.

If it's practical, give visitors an opportunity to make money by being an affiliate of yours – paying any visitor who wants to sign up a commission for sales they generate for you. Affiliate pioneer Amazon.com has tens of thousands of salespeople in cyberspace working on commission selling books!

One last type of content that no site should overlook is the offer to provide new, regular information to the visitor through e-mail. For the best response, make them feel special, and make the offer seem valuable. For example, 'If you want to hear about our new products and money-saving specials, just type your e-mail address below to become one of our Gold Service Members. You'll get unadvertised discounts, the first look at new lines, and insider advice on creative ways to use our fine products.'

The alternate-choice close

The best way to make a sale is to limit the buyer's choices. An alternate-choice close presents the customer with a simple choice; regardless of which choice the customer makes, the sale is closed: 'Will that be cash or charge?' 'Do you want that in yellow or blue?' 'Would delivery tomorrow be OK, or would Friday be better?' Studies have shown that if you ask simple yes/no questions, you're likely to get a 'No,' but if you offer customers a clear, simple choice, they are very likely to choose one of the options you offer, and you make the sale.

Designing web sites to maximise press relations

We have arrived in the digital age in which most journalists turn to the web first for basic corporate information. About half begin by visiting a target company's web site; the rest turn to search engines. This finding demonstrates the necessity of a corporate web site with a clearly labelled Press or PR section that quickly satisfies journalists' basic needs. Of particular note is the importance of solid representation in external search engines and databases. Run a test yourself. Try Google. Key in the name of a client, company, or executive and see what kind of digital trail appears. So what does a reporter want from that initial web site contact?

1. find a PR contact
2. check basic facts, spellings, ages of executives, location of headquarters, etc
3. discover the company's slant on events
4. download images to illustrate stories.

This material should be easy to find (no passwords or registration) and should be cleansed of corporatese. Some tips to improve the usability of a corporate web site's PR area include:

● Start with an internal audit, taking a hard look at your site while bearing in mind the report's guidelines.
● Take a look at your web site's online PR information section to see how well it supports the four basic needs outlined above. Will a journalist, working on deadline, find the answers on your site?
● Consider conducting your own usability survey with friendly reporters.

With Kodak CDs, you can do things you never thought you could! With Kodak Programmable CD-ROM Technology, businesses can build 1:1 communications with customers using the power of customised multimedia. And each disc can be unique with a secure serial number and virtually impenetrable anti-piracy protection for uses such as e-debit cards, personalised e-catalogue and online membership cards. To learn more, visit **www.kodak.com/go/cdprom**

The best websites:

- **Load in about 10 seconds at 28.8 Kbps**: Your designers may have DSL or cable modems, but 93 percent of your customers don't. The bottom line is that nobody is going to wait more than 10 to 15 seconds for your page to appear.

- **Respect conventions**: Blue, underlined text means hyperlink, or 'Click here,' to almost everyone. Avoid underlining or using blue text for anything else. Place your navigation cues on the top or left of every page, with the same links arrayed at the bottom. Use categorisation schemes that make sense, e.g. a series of tabs for multiple elements.

- **Make everything obvious**: First and foremost, help your prospect see the information – white backgrounds are quick to download and help information stand out. Label stuff, and do so without jargon. Offer concise explanations.

- **Don't assume the client is an expert user**: Technology is a wonderful thing, but Mary and Fred Consumer are years behind the tech types. Therefore, your GUI should be simple (GUI – graphical user interface, pronounced 'gooey' the sort of stuff you won't want your prospects stuck in). Also, never make them download plug-ins. Average shoppers don't know how, and even if they do, why take them away from the shopping process and force them to do something else? If you can't design it into your site and still have it load quickly and do all that other important stuff, leave it out. And give your prospects simple, clear instructions and helpful tools to guide them through the buying process.

> Here's what the top 100 web sites have in common - fast download times; few graphics; little, if any, multimedia; no frames; similar navigation systems; high-contrast text with lots of white space; most links in 'traditional' blue, underlined text; no background imagery; very few obvious JavaScript tricks; no DHTML; no splash pages; and a solid database-powered back-end.

Writing for the internet

We shouldn't think that text on the web is just re-jigged print material squirted through an HTML word processor. In a printed piece, we see the shape of a story. We can flip a few pages ahead. We can scan brochure copy. But browsing a web site doesn't provide the same orientation. We may be looking at the whole story in 20 lines. Or it may be just the beginning of an HTML trek running 100K or more. We can scroll top to bottom before we ever start reading, and there's no guarantee that the writer won't jump to another page with a hyperlink in the last paragraph. We need to get a glimpse of the structure from the printed page. The web is a new medium without limits and it's up to the writer to provide the structure that helps readers find their way.

Good web writing is somewhat didactic. You have to telegraph the outline of the narrative in the first few sentences or diagram it in a set of hyperlinked heads and subheads at the top of the page. Following paragraphs should be short and packed with information. They should be written in the active voice and waste no bytes on rambling subordinate clauses. Editorial content is still the chief method of communicating on the web and the demand for quality content is growing.

It is important to understand the physical parameters of the medium. Resolution and eye tracking are two key issues. Text on the web is published in low resolution. Think about reading the next issue of your favourite magazine on your television in 72 dpi (dots per inch) in 10-point Times New Roman font. It's uncomfortable and hurts the eyes. In fact, the web and the PC monitor, even those new flat-screen, hi-res monitors, are basically windows, not pages. The web is not a book, magazine, or newspaper. It is, more accurately, an illustrated screen, a window to another world, with text. To avoid discomfort, we must keep browsers/visitors stimulated with movement, keep them flitting from short blocks of large, high-impact sans-serif text that gets right to the point. The most effective web material keeps readers constantly engaged with interactivity through a series of structured, interlacing hyperlinks and bookmarks.

Text is still the basic building block of the web. Content is still king. A well-conceived, well-written and well-edited page or document is easier to read on the web, as elsewhere. Text is also an aid to orient the reader's navigational system. So how do we greet these visitors to our web sites? Since we often cannot control how visitors arrive, we should include some basic text at the top of every web page to orient our guests. Microcontent is a new web tool and includes headlines, subheads, linking text, navigation-bar text, and so on. It should be self-explanatory and should provide context. It should answer these questions:

? Whose site is this?
? What kinds of information does this page contain?
? How much information is on this page?
? Who is this information intended for?

Microcontent must consist of little pearls of clarity – no more than 40 to 60 characters to explain the macrocontent. Microcontent should clearly explain what an article is about in terms that relate to the user. Unless the title or subject makes it absolutely clear what the page or the email is about, users will not open or read it. Microcontent serves as a billboard for macrocontent. Write in plain language. Do not use teasers to entice people to click to find out what a story is about. In print, curiosity gets people to turn the page or to start reading an article; online, the wait can be too painful.

Editing the written word is important. A few guiding principles:

- Take advantage of the structural opportunities that hypertext or hyperlinks offer, but don't get carried away. Use hypertext to break pieces of a document off, to separate subpages or to make connections to other pages on the site (or outside the site) to add context or depth.

- Write your own microcontent, including the text for navigation within the document. Don't leave this important task to the web designer; don't leave any text decisions to the designer. Microcontent is an editorial issue. If you're writing about new software, write your own subheads for the sections (or subpages), then add a collection of links at the top of each page that corresponds to the heads and subheads. The links function as a summary of the piece and allow one to jump to the desired section.

- It's important to understand when redundancy in web content is and is not OK. If a text-based work is divided on multiple web pages, any one of which theoretically may be accessed first by the visitor, you may have to repeat some information from page to page. Just don't force readers to jump around too much and lose their place.

- Never bury your lead. Web users are notoriously flighty. Don't make people wade through background to eventually arrive at your point. They won't follow you.

- Tight writing is best. Ditch prepositional phrases. Avoid the passive voice, and be sensitive to tone and flow. But don't edit so tightly that your writing becomes choppy and abrupt and interferes with readability.

Headlines

The headline is the most important part of your sales copy. Whether your audience is looking at an ad, a web page, or a sales letter, if your headline doesn't capture attention you won't sell a thing. You need a powerful headline for everything you write, and maybe more than one! A powerful headline must capture your audience's attention by telling them what's in it for them with potent words.

POTENT WORDS			
You	How	Save	Free
Numbers	Original	Sure	Image
Results	Proven	Confidence	Economical
Now	Today	Latest	Quality
Satisfaction	Outstanding	Immediate	Successful
Discover	Value	Instant	Money-making
Personal	Guarantee	Secret	New
Giant			

Different media have different length limits. A website title should be no more than seven words or a good rule of thumb is:

**Never have a headline longer than
two lines of text**

**'Putting your headline in quotes or using a question mark
at the end can also help, don't you think?'**

Determine the main benefit you want to convey to your audience. Are you going to save them time? Tell them how much time. Are you going to help them make money? How much money? For a truly effective headline, use the word 'you' at least once. Perfect headlines are not easy to create but the best way to learn is to study the masters. Tabloids are a good place to look. Collect headlines that capture your attention, study them, and try to mimic them.

- A page of text, whether online or off, looks dull unless it is broken up with bullet points and subheadings. Bullet points and subheadings are often what people read first.
- You can use subheadings to keep your audience interested in your text. Condense the benefits you will be explaining in the text into a few words and use it as a subheading. When people see benefits they're interested in, they'll stop to read the rest of your document. Keep telling them you will tell them things they want to know and they'll read your text.

How to obtain the secrets of the best websites

To view the source code on a website you like the look of ...
you can do this in Internet Explorer by choosing the View menu and selecting Source. In Netscape, choose the View menu and select Page Source.

To copy and paste their source code into your word processing program ...
the best way is to click at the top of the document, then scroll to the bottom of the document and press shift while clicking with your mouse at the lower right hand corner. This should highlight all the text in the Source Code window. Press Ctrl and C at the same time to copy the text. Open your word processing program. You should be able to paste the Source Code into a new document by starting a new document and pressing Ctrl and V at the same time. If it doesn't work, look for a Paste function under your Edit menu.

To find out how many times they use keywords ...

this is simple in most advanced word processing programs. Use the Find/Replace function to replace each keyword with itself. The program will tell you how many replacements it made. Make a note of how often each word was used. If you're interested in search phrases (and you should be), also note whether the words you are looking at are often near each other. Then do a word count. There is also probably a Word Count option in your program. In Microsoft Word, it's in the Tools menu. Select it to find out how many words there are in the document.

Divide the number of keywords by the number of total words to discover their keyword density, then try to duplicate that percentage on your page by inserting or deleting keywords in your document.

Making the most of keywords

Keywords and key phrases are the cornerstone of search engine positioning and optimisation. If you want your web pages to show up in the first screenful (or two) of results at a major search engine, you must focus your page content and HTML tags on words and phrases you have chosen carefully for just that purpose. When visitors query a search engine such as AltaVista, they type in keywords they think will produce the kind of pages they want, e.g. cricket balls. The engine organises its results according to its estimation of each page's relevancy, based on the keywords and keyword phrases it found when it spidered the site. Each search engine has its own method for evaluating relevancy and ranking results. This algorithm is based on factors such as how often the searched-for keyword(s) appear on the page; how the keywords are used; and where they are positioned within the page, or in relation to each other.

Let's suppose you have a web site designed to sell fluorescent skate boards, and you want to get some traffic from major search engines. You might think it would make sense to choose 'skate boards ' as a keyword phrase to work on. Even if we assume a more skilful search using advanced syntax, you'll see that an exact phrase search on 'skate boarding' could turn up literally thousands of pages, while a Boolean AND search will shows up even more. The goal in choosing keywords and key phrases for search engine optimisation is to find terms that your target audience is likely to use at a search site, and that are precise enough to limit the competition for top placement. Here's a better keyword phrase to work with: 'fluorescent skate boards for the cool twenty-something trend-setter'. Your keywords must be the focus of your page in order to gain top ranking in the search engines. Most people search the internet using phrases rather than words. Choose your keywords with that in mind. Focusing on less popular phrases and misspellings of commonly misspelled words will make it easier to reach top ten listings in the search engines.

Start revolutionising your website by making sure keywords appear in the text of each web page. The text, especially headings and links, is the best place for you to put keywords. All search engines look at your page's headings, links, and the first and last paragraphs of text for keywords. Words in headings and links are considered more heavily in search queries than any other words on your page.

Try to work keywords naturally into your sentences and include them in bulleted lists. Keywords organised in phrases throughout your text will give your website better relevance for those phrases in search engines. Including keyword phrases at the beginning and end of your document gives them added relevance.

Do not list a keyword multiple times on a single line, or list keywords the same colour as your background. Most search engines consider such tactics spamming, and will penalise your site by lowering your rankings or dropping your website from their listing entirely. Try to make each keyword equal three to eight percent of the text on your page. The more keywords, the higher you rank, until the search engine begins to think there are too many of a particular keyword. Search engines, especially Alta Vista, will penalise your site by lowering your rankings for using too high a keyword weight. After you have keywords in your text, list them as phrases in metatags and design a page description including as many keywords as possible. Make sure your description also sells your website – it will be your only chance to attract visitors through search engines and directories.

Your description should be listed in a meta tag, a comments tag within your Head tag, an alternative text tag behind one of your graphics, and in your text – preferably the first text on your page. The repetition will ensure that every major search engine uses it as the description of your site, rather than a random section of text from your page. Next, distil your description down to between five and seven words, perhaps including your company name, for the title of your webpage. The keywords you include in your title should be the most important words on your page. Many people will make a decision on whether to visit your website based solely upon these words, and search engines regard them as pretty important as well.

Some research on search engine algorithms indicates that a fewer number of keywords may help you better target the most important search if you're working to increase your page's ranking on the search engines. Consider using both lowercase and capitalised forms of your most important words, since some search engines are capitalisation-specific. Make sure that you don't repeat any word more than three times so you're not penalised for keyword spamming.

Tips for using keywords in search engine ranking:

- Start with the type of page you have. Be sure the industry type, the name of the business, and the names of your products are listed as keywords on at least one of your webpages, e.g. book publishers might be listed under publishing, books, their name, and the specific titles of their books.
- Next, think of synonyms for your industry and product types. For example, an internet-related page might want to be listed under webpages, websites, internet, and online.
- Think about your audience. Who will be coming to your web site? If you were one of those people, how would you ask the search engine to find a company like yours? If possible, ask people in your target audience what they would search for.
- Ask yourself, 'Are my keywords and phrases common?' Try searching for your keyword phrases. If you get relevant responses in the tens or hundreds of thousands, try something else.
- Consider using your city or county with common keywords. If you have a special niche in your industry, use that. Use the name of the company owner or other prominent employees – people often search for specific names.
- There will be less competition to fight against for top search engine listings when you use unusual keyword phrases. Maybe you can't get the top spot for marketing, but you can for 'choosing keywords.' Look for phrases associated with your business that you could write a webpage about.
- If your web site has several pages, attempt to get them all in search engines, focusing on different keyword phrases for each page.
- If you focus on just a few keyword phrases for each page, you will be able to rank higher for all of your keyword phrases: you can afford to weight the keyword phrases more heavily in each document and keep

your documents shorter. You'll get more traffic with one page in the top ten search results of five keyword phrases than five pages in the top ten search results of one keyword phrase.

- Keyword phrases should evolve with your website, so don't feel bad if you don't rank highly to start with. Search for your keyword phrases on the top seven search engines. Lycos, AltaVista, HotBot, Webcrawler, Infoseek, Northern Light and Excite are the most important. Yahoo! is a directory.

- For more ideas, check out the Document Source of your competitors' websites. Consider using the same words they do in their meta tags (if they have any). Give the words your own twist, add more, or use them more frequently to rank higher.

- Directories will let you tell them the keywords you want to be associated with, but search engines look at your site to determine under which queries your website will appear. Most people start looking for information on the internet using search engines.

The best way to get great results on every search engine is to have good keyword density in your title tag, heading tags, link tags, and meta description. Just to make sure, you should also have good keyword density in your visible text and alternative text. Since this is so complicated, when doing your keyword density analysis, just count everything in a word processing program like Microsoft Word. Each search engine has its own 'magic' keyword density where pages will rank most highly. For obvious reasons, they try to keep this number a secret, but online marketers are endlessly testing to discover them. To keep search engine specialists on their toes, search engines constantly change these numbers without notice. If you go above the 'magic' keyword density, your website will be penalised. Early on, search engines figured out pages with too many keywords were likely lacking real content, and were often set up just to lure visitors somewhere else. They consider this kind of deception 'spamming' – just like junk email, they're junk websites. You will get better rankings by having a slightly lower density. For most of the big search engines, the 'magic number' is around 7 percent, but you could get good rankings with as little as 1 percent for less common keywords and phrases.

Try calculating your keyword density for one of your pages. If your density is less than 1 percent or higher than 7 percent, you know right now why you aren't ranking as high as you'd like.

You don't really need to know the magic keyword density to get the best rankings in search engines for a variety of keywords. You just need to do better than the competition, which is why it's easier to get and keep good rankings with less popular keywords. The best way to determine the keyword density you need for great rankings is to check the keyword density of pages already ranking well for the keywords you're interested in.

Keep tabs on your competitors online. How are they ranked in search engines compared to you?

Try doing a search for some of your keywords. Visit the website at the top of the list or the third or fourth for really competitive keywords – the highest-ranking websites may be disguising their source code or sending something else to search engines.

13 Questions for website designers

Does the look and feel of the site seem ethical?

People don't know you from Adam. But they might have come up against a lot of Arthur Daleys and that makes them wary of you and your products or services. How do you convince them to trust you? It means looking professional, not like a site put together by amateurs. It means having policies, which are and sound ethical. If you offer a money-back guarantee, don't hedge or fill it so full of caveats that it sounds dishonest. Your promises must not only be honest; they must sound honest, too.

Are you making it hard for visitors to print out information from your web site?

The worst offenders are web pages that use white or light lettering on a dark background – the printed pages are almost solid ink. If the page has graphics, navigation aids, or other material not useful to your visitor on a printed page, consider creating a link to a full text page formatted for a printer. Make sure all of your company information is on the printed page for easy reference.

Does the site treat visitors like individuals?

Online visitors see themselves like single shoppers who have dropped into your jewellery shop and find they are the only customer in the place. They want to be treated with all the patience, consideration, and personalised attention that you would devote to them in your real-world shop. The more you can make them feel special, the more they will like you, and want to buy from you. If you treat them like a number, they'll treat you the same way.

Is the overall layout of the homepage and other pages clean, organised and professional?

Most of your visitors will only know you from your web site. What kind of impression will it make on them? You can dress your site to look businesslike, casual, etc. Like your clothing, the way you dress your site will create a strong first impression of your company and its products.

Does the site seem information rich?

Research shows that most adults visit web sites for information. Information rich sites score highest on 'must bookmark' and 'will return' scales. Those are two critical factors for creating new and repeat business. An information-rich site is one, which provides helpful ideas, facts, recommendations, stories, humour, entertainment, contests, and other content which visitors will find interesting. The opposite of an information-rich site is one, which does nothing but pitch your product or service, or just looks like your brochure.

Are the pages so wide that visitors have to scroll sideways?

People don't like to scroll anyway, but they especially dislike scrolling sideways because they don't keep all of the information in the same paragraph on screen. It is also wise not to force visitors to scroll down too far, say over two screens, especially if the navigation buttons and menus are at the top.

Can visitors immediately tell who you are and what you offer?

Having your name, brand, slogan, and type of product(s) at the top of the homepage gives you an opportunity for another branding impression, just like your shop's name above the door. It is a good idea on your homepage to list the various ways people can get in touch with you e.g. address, phone, fax, e-mail, etc. All some people want to know is where to send their order or who to call for a catalogue. Make it easy for people to tell you what they want.

Does the site tell visitors that the company recognises their motives for dropping in, and wants to help?

If you are looking for maternity clothes, what do you want to see first when you approach a maternity wear shop? A sign that says, 'We have a huge variety of styles and sizes.' That sign tells you the shop owner knows the clothes you want will not be like most other women's, they must be in a particular style and size. It also tells you that their big selection means you'll probably find what you're looking for. Your web site is like a maternity wear shop. Your visitors are looking for special information. And they won't stay one second longer than they have to if they don't think you've got it. After all, some other virtual shop is just on the other side of a click. Knowing their buying motives tells you what to say at the top of your homepage. For example, if they want to grow their business, your first words might be 'Looking for some great ways to grow your business? You're in the right place! We have hundreds of ways to help you make money!' The trick is simple: Just stimulate their desire, and then promise to satisfy it.

Can visitors get to where they want to be within 3 clicks?

Visitors will give you two or three clicks to get them to the information they want. Then they will try somewhere else. Can they get to any page on your site in two or three clicks? If not, fix the problem. One way is to use more navigation options, or give them a drop down menu when their cursor moves over each of your basic navigation options.

Do you ask the visitor to place an order or make a call?

The most fundamental rule in selling is 'ask for the sale.' Your web site should do the same. You might be direct, like 'Click here to add this item to your shopping cart.' Or it might be more indirect, like 'Would you like to select a top to go with your jeans?' You might be asking for the order, or just for them to take the next step – 'Get more information on this offer. Click here now.' Researchers have found that using commands like 'click here' and telling them to do it 'now' increase the response rate. Banner ads that contain the words 'click here' get a better response, too. Remember, your site isn't a library. You want them to buy, not just browse. So ask them.

Do you have 128-bit encryption security for sales transactions?

This is the code word for the most secure type of transaction. Chances are your merchant account provider offers it. If so, tell your customers that you have '128-bit encryption security, the most secure way to use your credit card online.' Try to use the words security and secure several times.

Do you ask for their e-mail address?

If you have an e-commerce site, research shows that the average consumer will come back six times before buying something from you for the first time. You shouldn't rely on the chance that they'll remember to find you again. Get their e-mail address so you can remind them. Ask for it, and then promise to give them something in return. They are doing you a favour, and trusting you, so you should provide a reward that will make them feel good about your company. Information, like an Insider Report, is always a good bet, as are discounts, free samples, and contest entries. You want to build a positive, personal relationship with them. Don't lose a possible customer by asking for too much. And don't lose a possible customer by failing to get their address.

Is the site designed to satisfy your targeted customers' buying motives?

The two most dangerous assumptions of most internet marketers are: if I build it, they will come and everyone is my customer. Who are your customers? What kind of content do they expect to find on your site? Keep in mind the purpose of your site: Is it an online sales brochure, a newsletter or magazine site, or a tool to sell your products? The answer will help determine what content you should include in it. They won't come unless you have a strong online and offline marketing program – one that promises them something they want. And once they show up in your virtual shopfront, they must see at once that you have what they want. People want different things, even when buying the same product. Teenage boys want something different in skateboards to the twenty-something trendsetter. If you tried to sell to teenage boys using the same pitch you successfully used for twenty-something, it wouldn't work. Whatever your goals, be sure the site is specifically designed for each of your specific customers, not some general, nebulous group of everyone on the internet.

4

Marketing Through
Search Engine Optimisation

CLICK-ONS

Preparing outstanding descriptions

META tags

Gateway pages

Getting ranked high

Submitting pages to directories

Paying a service

Customising error messages

Preparing outstanding descriptions

Prepare to submit your site to search engines by fine-tuning your site description. Your site description should be able to sell your website to potential visitors in three sentences or less. It isn't enough to just have links on the top search engines and directories. You must convince people to visit your site. A good description can sell your site better than the top spot in search engine results! First, make sure your site description has an offer potential visitors will not be able to pass up, e.g. a contest, discount, free report, or rare item can bring rivers of visitors to your site. Then, follow up on the offer! Remember to include your most important keywords and phrases in your description. Keywords in your description have added weight with search engines, and since you will be repeating your description several times, the keywords and phrases you include will have greater frequency as well.

Once you have the perfect offer, and the site content to back it up, make sure the search engines will pick up your description and use it. If your visitors know you have quality content, they will be more likely to visit your website. If you already have your description in meta tags, that's a good start. Unfortunately for website designers, not all search engines look at meta tags. Infoseek and Lycos ignore all meta tags as spam devices.

If you want your site listed on Infoseek and Lycos with your description intact, put your description as close to the top of your website as possible. Use a comments tag or hidden input tag within the Head tag, right after your meta tags.

Repeat your description as alternative text to a graphic at the top left of your webpage, and/or as the first text of your document. This description should come directly after your body tag. If you do not want visitors to see your description on your website, and you don't have any graphics to hide it under, you can create an invisible graphic. Simply make a graphic out of a period (.) the same colour as your background to place at the top left of your document.

Every search engine recognises visible text, and puts special emphasis on heading and link tags. The best place to put your description for search engine spiders is where every visitor will see it at the top of your page in a heading or link tag, either before or directly after your page title. Your page title should be visible on your website! Make it a headline designed to pull visitors into the page and put it at the top, so visitors will know they've arrived at the right place.

There is no 'magic spot' you can put your website description where every search engine will find it. Let the design of your webpage determine where the description should appear, not the spiders. Your visitors are your most important resource, and not all of them will be coming from search engines. Create a description, which will compel people to visit your site.

Putting that description where search engines will find it will mark you as a professional, and encourage search engine users to pass by pages with better placement to visit you.

AVOID ...

- using the same or similar colours for text and background

- tiny text website visitors will have difficulty reading

- repetition of keywords in close proximity in your body text and image alt text

- repetition of keywords in your meta tags - some search engines reward this, but HotBot will penalise you

- meta redirection to a new page in less than 15 seconds

- submitting more than five different pages to the same search engine during one day

- submitting any page more than once to the same search engine during one day

- .nu domains - they are often used by adult sites. Alta Vista has banned them, and other engines may follow suit.

META tags

Prepare to submit your website to search engines by adding meta tags. Meta tags are instructions for search engine spiders which should be placed between the <HEAD> and </HEAD> tags of an HTML document – usually after your page title. They will not appear in your visitors' browsers (they're 'invisible' tags). You can (and should) include your website description in one, your keywords in another, and perhaps have a third to provide other instructions to a spider or browser.

It's important to design your website so that each webpage includes a clear page title since when your site shows up on a search engine, the webpage title will be displayed. This isn't the headline that you place between HTML <H1> tags, but the title placed between HTML <TITLE> tags. The title of each page ought to be both descriptive as well as provocative. For example, 'Tony's Training Academy' might be better titled

'Tony's Training Academy Have Won Five International Awards for Quality Delivery.' Think of the webpage title as a vital marketing tool.

The description META tag is used by some search engines as the sentence or two they display below your webpage title. Limit this to about 200 characters or so. The keywords META tag will include half dozen to several dozen words that someone might search on in order to find your website. There's both science and old wives tales that contribute to META tag lore. You can learn at Danny Sullivan's SearchEngineWatch.com (**www.searchenginewatch.com/webmasters/**).

Add meta tags to all the pages in your web site. Influencing the key words and descriptions search engines associate with your website can significantly increase your traffic. There are four types of meta tags that are especially useful: description, keywords, refresh and robots. The format is as follows:

1   <meta name='description' content='your page description here.'> This is the description most search engines will use for your site, so make sure it sells.

2   <meta name='keywords' content='enter keyword phrases here'> These are additional words the search engine will associate with your web site.

3   <meta HTTP-EQUIV='refresh' content='18;URL=http://www.yoursite. com/'> This tag allows you to send your visitors to a different page. '18' is the number of seconds the browser will wait before sending visitors to the new web page. This is great for doorway pages and pages directing visitors when you moved a page, but watch out: some search engines won't index the page if the refresh time isn't long enough (try least 18 seconds).

4   <meta name='robots' content='noindex, nofollow'> This tag will tell search engine spiders not to index your page and/or follow its links. With the robots tag, you can specify either 'noindex,' 'nofollow,' or both. <meta name='revisit-after' content='12 days'> This tag will tell search engine spiders come back to index your page every 12 days. You can specify any number of 'days.'

A few more tips:

●   Rely on your page content and title tag to raise your relevancy, rather than repeating words in your meta tag. Also, avoid repetitions of one keyword – or versions of that keyword – placed next to itself, even if it's spelled differently. Search engines are more likely to notice, and lower your ranking, or drop your page entirely.

- Use description and keyword meta tags on pages you want the search engines to list. Use the robots meta tag on all the pages you don't want the search engine spiders to index. Remember not all search engines support this meta tag – a robots.txt file excluding pages or directories from spidering are more effective (AltaVista's search submission help files explain how to create a robots.txt file). Tags are not case-sensitive, but the content of tags may be – depending on the search spider.

- Some search engines are case-sensitive, others aren't. Some search engines use 'stemming,' meaning when they see a word in your meta tag, like 'yell,' they will also cite you in results for 'yells,' 'yelling,' and 'yeller.' Other search engines will see 'yelling' and cite you in results for 'yell.' A few search engines will only cite your website in results for the exact word and spelling you have listed. It's better to be safe than sorry, so either include everything or create a doorway page to cater to each search engine.

- Don't put commas between keywords and phrases. Eliminating commas gives you extra space for alternative spellings and capitalisations of your key words, since search engines only look at a certain number of characters in your meta tags (this number is different for each search engine, so always add the most important words first). Without commas, some search engines will also keep all the words together in their database, allowing searchers to find your website under more word combinations.

- Use a description in your meta tags (preferably repeated in your text) designed to sell your web site contents. Keyword phrases should definitely be used in the description when possible, and describe your page.

- Different search engines handle meta tags in different ways, and there is a wide range of opinion on how often you should repeat words and how long your tags should be. However, when keywords are listed in close proximity in the meta tag, you will almost always rank higher when people search for the words together. Don't repeat words with the same spelling in your tag, and focus on just a few key phrases per page.

Gateway pages

Registering your site with the search engines is the first step. But with tens of millions of webpages, your site may hardly be visible. These days you may need to construct a series of gateway pages, each tuned for a particular search phrase and search engine. Then fine-tune these gateway pages to rank high using a program such as WebPosition Gold (**www.webposition.com/ d2.pl?r=AQH-55E7**). Many small businesses outsource search engine positioning because of the considerable time investment it requires.

While it's wise to design your webpages to score high on search engines, you don't want to make your content subject to the changing vagaries of search engine preferences. Instead, you build a series of gateway webpages that point to your main website. Sometimes these gateway pages may employ an HTML frame system that contains your main webpage within it. That way the words in one frame of the system can be altered without changing the content of your main webpages. Let's say you wanted to show up in the top 10 of a search for the key phrase 'conservatory blinds.' Since each major search engine has different and sometimes conflicting algorithms, you need to build a separate webpage fine-tuned for 'conservatory blinds ' for each search engine, perhaps 6 to 10 different gateway pages per keyword or key phrase. If you desire to score high for several search words or phrases, you'll need to create a set of gateway pages for each. Then throw in the complication that algorithms often change. Furthermore, you need to be careful, since some search engines have been known to ban domain names or IP addresses associated with search engine spamming. Consequently these gateway pages may be hosted on a domain other than your primary website.

Here's how you can get the focused power of gateway pages:

- Make sure each page of your site focuses on only a few keyword phrases e.g. three.
- Once you've chosen the proper keyword phrases, put them in your meta keyword and description tags. Use your most important keyword phrase in the title of the page. If you have images on your page, add the keyword phrases as alternative text. Put them in headlines and create links using them as a description.
- Now you're ready for the body copy. If the webpage is an article, you already have text. Otherwise, you may have to write some. The text of each webpage should be at least 100 words and include each keyword phrase at least twice. If you are working with an article, make sure it uses the keyword phrases – a little rewriting may be necessary, but keep it sounding natural.
- Submit the webpages you have optimised directly to the major search

engines. Not Alta Vista or Northern Light – just submit your main page and let them find your other pages. Remember to check your listings in a couple of weeks. Make sure your page got listed and is getting the ranking you wanted.

- If you are still having trouble getting good listings, especially on one or two search engines, consider tweaking the page to rank better. Find out what that search engine is looking for in a webpage, and create a new version of your page based on that information. Your new page will be a gateway page.

Getting ranked high

There are five successful ways to get a site ranked high by search engines:

- **Hotboosting**: This tactic can be used on certain search engines where, if you don't get any clicks, you disappear. So you have to go to it yourself and click on it. You don't want to do it a million times because search engines know what you are doing and they know your IP address. But if you do it every so often, it can help.
- **Link assassinations**: If somebody is ranked above you in a search engine and they are using spam tactics to get there, you can report them to the search engines so they disappear and you usually move up in rank.
- **Page mirroring**: You need informational pages targeting specific keywords. However, each one will work on certain engines and not others. So, you can create a very similar page targeting the same keyword but it's built in a way to appeal to a particular search engine. You only submit that page to that one search engine so the others won't frown on you for spamming.
- **Meta tags**: Bad meta tags are ones using vague terms like 'business'. You need to be really specific with meta tags – this is your niche, your description. Also, make sure you put the most important keyword in front so if the engine clips the description short, the important words are still there.
- **Link popularity**: Some search engines rank you according to how many other domains link to your domain. You're not looking for visitors to find you at the other site, the only thing you're looking for that page to do is have a search engine spider it. The engines give you points for link quality. A quality link is worth much more than lots of non-quality links. So, you need to find people who will trade links with you.

While important, just registering your webpages with the search engines isn't likely to lift you above the clutter of billions of webpages currently on the internet. If your site doesn't appear in the top 10 or top 20 results for a search, your site will seldom be visited. To achieve high ranking, you need to enter the complex world of search engine optimisation (SEO) or search engine positioning. To do this, consider using a submission service such as Submit-It **http://submitit.linexchange.com** or All4one Submission Machine **www.all4one.com/all4submit**. The most important search engines that robotically 'spider' or index your site are: AltaVista, Excite, HotBot, Lycos, Infoseek, WebCrawler, and Northern Light.

> Yahoo is the most important listing of all though it's technically a directory, rather than a search engine. It uses real humans to read your 200 character sentence, so be careful, and follow their instructions. **www.yahoo.com/docs/info/include.html**

Maintaining search engine positions

Four things you should do to keep your rankings high:

1   Don't rewrite any of your highly ranked pages or make other drastic changes. Try to keep your keyword weight (the percentage of search terms in your text), file name, and keyword prominence (use of search terms in your headings, links, and meta tags) the same. This is not to say you shouldn't update your pages with new information. Letting your page content stagnate could cause some of your search engine rankings to slip. As long as you don't change the number or prominence of your key search terms, changing the content of your website should not affect your ranking.

2   A search engine position analyser, like WebPosition or TopDog **www.topdog.com** would save you time and help manage your search engine submissions. WebPosition focuses on the top 15 search engines, and will also critique a webpage's relevance to the search terms you want to rank well for by each search engine's criteria (that they analyse). You should know how well your webpage will rank before submitting it.

3   TopDog checks almost 200 search engines, and will submit your website to over 100. Many marketers think it's the best because it analyses and submits to the most search engines.

4   Check your rankings regularly – at least once a week. Make sure your
    page isn't dropped or beaten out by the competition.

> You can also check your website's ranking in search engines manually
> by bookmarking the results of searches for your keywords, or use a
> free tool on the internet (Jim Tools **http://jimtools.com**).

Being at the top of the search engine heap makes your website a prime target
for webmasters trying to figure out how to get prime rankings themselves.
They will visit your website and try to find out how you got those rankings.
Then they'll improve on it. The more popular the search term you've
mastered is, the more quickly somebody else will submit a website that
earns an even better ranking. Sometimes the search engine will notice that
they're using some kind of trick and drop them.

One thing you can do to protect yourself is simply to put in some white
space before you begin the html code for each webpage. Press the Enter key
enough times to put two screens of blank grey in your visitor's screens when
they try to 'View Source.' Most visitors will think you have some html-
hiding trick and give up before scrolling down enough to find your code.
Other ways to hide your source code include programs, which hide your
html code from your visitors, while showing it to search engines.

A variation is a spamming code, which will show search engines
different stuff than browsers, allowing you to use very keyword-heavy
search engine text to get good rankings while showing visitors something
completely different. When your page is dropped, resubmit it (or a page
linking to it in Alta Vista, which ranks pages it 'finds' better) as quickly as
possible. It can take over two months to get listed on some search engines!

Keep track of which pages you submitted and when, then check and
make sure they are re-added to the search engine's database on schedule. If
they haven't been, you'll need to submit them again. If you don't keep track,
you may submit your page too often and get penalised. Look for related
websites to link to you. More and more search engines are using link
popularity to rank websites. Too much search term repetition in your
document, and it may be penalised. Links are one good thing you can't have
too much of. Links are harder for other websites to duplicate than keyword
weight and prominence in your source code. They also bring visitors of their
own to your website, making you less dependent on search engine traffic.

Free search engine submission tools

Dream Submit: **www.dreamsubmit.net/stack** - Submission to over 50 search engines

Web Source: **www.web-source.net** - A quick site submission tool and directory

---

Submitting pages to directories

Search engines are vital, but directories drive as much or more traffic to your site. And increasingly, search engines are combined with directories, so they'll include information from both human edited directories as well as automatically indexed webpages. The most important directory by far in most countries of the world is Yahoo (**www.yahoo.com**). But they are very picky about what they'll include in a listing. You'll also want a listing in the DMOZ Open Directory Project (**www.dmoz.org**) since HotBot, Lycos, and Netscape Search also use its material. A third important directory is LookSmart (**www.looksmart.com**) – not because it gets a lot of hits itself, but because its listings feed into search results from MSN Search, Excite, AltaVista, iWon, and CCN.com. The other directory that you should submit to is Ask Jeeves! (**www.ask.com**).

There's an important distinction between search engines and directories. A search engine is an automated indexing system that periodically sends a robotic 'spider' to your website to 'crawl', e.g. scan and index some or all of your webpages. Spiders can be complicated programs. Some will add your whole website to a search engine's database within a few days of submission (such as Northern Light). Some will add the first three levels (anything within three links from your home page), but take years to do so (such as Alta Vista). Others will seem to add pages randomly from your website (such as HotBot). Directories and a few search engines do not use spiders at all. They will only add pages that are submitted. However, that does not mean you should add all the pages of your website. You could be penalised for doing so. To make things a little more complicated, some search engines will not accept multiple submissions from the same domain during the same day. For example, Alta Vista will only accept up to five URLs in one session. A directory, on the other hand, is a listing describing your website edited by humans. In order to get on the search engines' radar you need to register your webpages.

Directories are the low-maintenance version of search engines. They put your website into a category, usually in alphabetic order, and sometimes give an option of searching as well. They rely on the information you provide when you submit your website, rather than actually visiting it, so you don't have to design your website with them in mind. For directories, it helps to have a website title starting with a letter or symbol at the top of the ASCII alphabet. Since the description is your only opportunity to sell your website to potential visitors, it had better sell your website and include as many keywords as possible. Get your home page listed only in directories which are extremely popular (like Yahoo) and any which specialise in your business or locality. The others probably aren't worth the effort to find them.

Every search engine is different. Directories and many search engines will only accept your main page. It should be called 'index,' 'home,' or 'default.' Webcrawler, Go, and Magellan will not accept more than that. Some search engines (like Alta Vista and Northern Light) will only want you to submit one page, and their 'spider' will crawl your website, adding your other pages to their database more or less randomly. Websites added to the database in this manner will get better ranking than pages submitted directly, but will be added more slowly. For these search engines, create a website directory, with links to all the pages you want indexed by search engines. This way, the spider only has to 'crawl' one level of your website.

Other search engines, including Hot Bot, Lycos, Direct Hit, MSN, and Excite, will allow you to submit more than one page without risk of banishment. MSN will accept up to five pages from any one domain per day. That is probably a good rule to follow for any search engine.

Which pages of my website should I submit to search engines?

Submitting multiple pages to the more liberal search engines will help you get more of your important pages in the search engines quickly. Since search engines occasionally get unhappy if you submit too many pages, you should only submit special pages:

- Pages with your most important keywords
- 'Index' pages that have links to a lot of your other pages, e.g. gateway pages
- Pages that you expect to bring you a lot of traffic or business e.g. Request Our Free Report

The most important thing is to create a page with links to all of the other pages in your website. This page will be your gateway page. Submit this page to all the search engines.

There are other high-traffic search engines you may want to be listed with. Visit a free submission service or buy your own program. Resubmit your website to these search engines whenever your website undergoes a major overhaul.

When and where to submit your site

Everywhere you look, there are advertisements for website submission services and programs. They claim to submit your website to hundreds, or even thousands of search engines on the internet. Is it worth it to submit to all of them? Many of the successful small search engines specialise in a certain region, industry, or topic. Others use the databases of larger search engines to supplement the submissions sent directly to them, making it useless to submit your website to them if you're already listed on the bigger engines. The submission services or programs will send your URL and description to all the search engines they can find on the internet – whether they relate to your website's content or not. Only the really expensive services and programs will target specific search engines and send descriptions and keywords formatted specifically for each one, submitting in a way the search engine will recognise as being from their website.

You may want to submit special pages to each search engine, designed to get you top listings. The good news is, for most topics and industries, you can still get listed in the top ten with keyword phrases of 2 - 3 words with minimal suffering.

The smaller content-specific search engines will be more difficult to find. Look for advertisements on web pages with similar content to yours and check the major search engines. Submit on their 'Add A Site' pages or with special software, which lets you submit your web pages to free for all links, directories, and search engines. If you find search engines, which apply to your region, industry, or topic, keep track of them with bookmarks or list their URLs. Resubmit your website whenever you make major changes.

> Check back with search engines in two months. By then, they should have several of your pages in their database. Check to see if your most important pages are listed. If not, submit them if the search engine allows multiple submissions from a website. NOTE: Their 'Add URL,' 'Submit a Site,' or 'Register a Site' page should have this information.

Algorithms and search engines

Every search engine has a complex method of determining which webpages come up as the top 10 choices when you put in a search word. Long gone are the days when you could repeat the words 'widget widget' 100 times hidden in white text at the bottom of your webpage and trick the engines into placing you in the number one spot. Now the placement algorithms or formulas are very complex and are constantly changing to outsmart the army of determined positioners vying for top positions on competitive keywords. The algorithms seem to include 'keyword density' in various sections of the webpage, the title, keyword META tag, the first 100 words of body text, headlines, etc.

> It is possible to do search engine optimisation yourself using WebPosition Gold (**www.webposition.com/d2.pl?r=AQH-55E7**). This software is constantly updated to provide you with the latest intelligence about changing search engine algorithms. Its Page Critic feature will analyse your webpages, compare them to top-scoring pages, and point out which elements to change to help you score higher on a particular search engine. In addition, you can use WebPosition Gold's automatic submission and reporting features to monitor your progress. The problem is that the amount of time required to maintain your position on competitive search words is considerable. And it must be sustained over a period of months as you submit, wait weeks for new rankings to appear, monitor your progress, make appropriate adjustments, and then resubmit again for a new cycle.

Paying a service

Because of the tedium and time investment involved in search engine optimisation, it is a good idea for smaller businesses to consider outsourcing this task to experts. You can find vendors in the Search Engine Placement

Improvement section of the Yahoo! directory. Be sure to ask for references and then contact them before you sign a contract. If possible, ask to have the gateway pages hosted on your own website under a domain name that you own, or you may find your hard-won positions disappear the moment you stop paying a monthly maintenance fee.

Parts of your website that search engines have elected most likely to succeed:

Your title

This is easily the most important part of your document. It can only be seven words, but needs to be the most important seven words on your page. Not only do search engines use your title as your most important keywords – visitors do, too! Visitors are likely to scroll down past any websites that don't use their keywords in their search engine results and just read the descriptions of those who do.

Headlines

Make sure your headlines use HTML heading tags to make them stand out to search engines. Headings and sub-headings are favourite places for search engines to look for keywords. They also help peak and maintain the interest of your visitors.

Your description

Some search engines don't read them at all, but they are important to search engine visitors as well as the search engines that do use them. Even if you get ranked well, if your keywords are not in your title and not in your description, you're not getting visitors.

First and last paragraphs

Almost all search engines index the first and last paragraphs of your website for keywords. They also might index the first word or two of your other paragraphs. The most important words here are the first words of your paragraphs. Put any keywords you are having trouble getting top rankings for right there.

Text link anchors

The blue text people can click on to visit another part of your website (or someone else's) is prime space for keywords. Unfortunately, search engines don't see alternative text for linked images the same way. This doesn't mean you have to use text links for all your navigational needs, however. You can just scatter a few links to other pages of your website among your text.

Customising error messages

Almost all website hosting companies will allow you to customise the error messages for your website. Your '404: Page Not Found' error could forward visitors to your home page. Server errors could give visitors a form to send you information about the problem, and unauthorised user errors could load a big 'KEEP OUT' sign. Customising your error messages will help you keep more visitors. Some visitors will always get error messages. There's nothing you can do to stop it. People will receive errors for any of the following reasons:

- they forgot their password or login name
- they want to see if they can get into a private section of your website with a bogus password and/or login name
- you mistyped a link on your website, or forgot to change a link to a deleted or renamed page
- they mistyped their password or login name
- one of your cgi scripts isn't working right
- your server is being overwhelmed with traffic, confused by your scripts, or just had one of those random errors computers are so famous for
- they bookmarked a page which you deleted or renamed.

What do they do when they get an error message? 99 percent of the time they go away, and they probably aren't coming back. Customising your error message gives you a chance to bring those lost visitors back into your website. It gives you a second chance to help them find what they want. Here's what you do: create a page that says what you want your visitors to see. You can create one page for all the errors, one for each error, or just create a page for '404: Page Not Found' errors, since they're the most common. Either use a 'meta redirect' tag and/or include:

- a link to your home page, and possibly the most popular pages on your website
- a site search engine, if you have one

- a message that says they have reached the wrong page, so they'll update their bookmarks
- an opportunity to email you about the problem.

Save the pages as normal HTML. Then, look at your online hosting manual for instructions on how to add the pages to your website. Some hosts make it easy – all you have to do is use a special name for your error pages. If the information is not in your online manual (or you don't have one), email technical support to ask them for instructions. Unix servers use a special file called '.htaccess' which gives the server instructions, such as which page to display for error messages. Just type something like 'ErrorDocument 404 /missing.html' where 'missing.html' is your error page and '404' is the type of error you want the page to display for. Use a new line for each error message you want to display. Save the file as Text Only and FTP it to your server in ASCII format. (Be sure to delete any '.txt' extension your program added to the file name.) Whenever you want to edit your error file, you can just open the HTML document you created and change it as you would any page of your website.

5

The Email Marketer

CLICK-ONS

The five Ws and an H

Communicating via email

Writing copy

Personalisation

Using autoresponders

Email lists

Capturing e-mail addresses

Using digital signatures

Using your email addresses

Direct mail

SPAM

Giving good email service

Reviewing your email communications

The five Ws and an H

Before you jump into the logistics of planning an email marketing campaign, ask some basic questions:

When?

When might the information you are conveying be useful? How often should you email updates about your product or service? Should you send reminders about an offer before it expires?

What?

What are you trying to accomplish? If it's to drive more traffic to your site, think again. That's not a business objective. Email marketing requires a good deal of planning as well as attention to detail. You need to be clear about your goal if you don't want to waste time and resources.

Why?

Why should they care? Your message must address the 'So what?' test. You're offering a free download of your software for a trial evaluation. Well, so is everyone else. Why is your download worth the recipient's time? If you can't answer the 'So what?' question, you're unlikely to get the response and results you're looking for.

Who?

With whom are you starting a conversation? Do you understand their business needs? Do you know how they think and what matters to them? Do you know how and why they use the web and email?

Where?

If your target readers are in their offices when they receive your message, you should focus your offer on the business benefits of your product or service, right? Wrong. People don't leave their emotions at the office door. B2B email recipients will respond to an offer such as 'Win a Palm Pilot,' even if it's unrelated to your product. Ask yourself where is each segment of your target audience in the buying or decision-making cycle?

How?

How do you want your audience to respond to your message? Are you just inviting click-throughs to a web site through embedded links? If you're selling a product, do you offer a phone number to reach a live salesperson?

If your message is the opening of a conversation, what other media can you use to extend that conversation long enough to make a sale?

Communicating via email

Your email campaign has an ultimate goal – more sales, subscribers, referrals, and so on. And it has an immediate goal – to get people to visit your web site. You're trying to persuade them to take the action you desire. Your list already accomplished the first step, prospecting, so your email now must build rapport, then qualify your prospect, present your offer, and close the sale – get prospects to take action. If your email doesn't perform all of those functions, it's going to fail most of the time.

> When you're selling face to face, only 7 percent of your communication is verbal; a full 93 percent is nonverbal! You assess your customers' appearance, tone of voice, facial expressions, eye contact, and gestures; and you manage your own. You can extend a pat on the back or a handshake. Perhaps most valuable, you have the opportunity to adjust your presentation based on your prospects' reactions. When selling via email, you and your prospect are invisible to each other. All you have are written words. You have to do 100 percent of the work with only 7 percent of the resources.

Communicating feelings

Just as in the real world, the tone of your communication is more important than its substance. Focus on your voice in the email, paying attention to the nuances of written language, e.g. word choice and phrasing, that accurately reflect the nuances in conversation and create an experience in the reader's mind that feels as close as possible to a real-world encounter. We may rationalise our buying decisions based on facts, but we make them based on feelings. Use colourful, feeling-ful words that stimulate the imagination. Once they're doing that, the leap to taking action is that much easier. The core feeling you're trying to create is enthusiasm and you generate enthusiasm by communicating your enthusiasm and if you're not excited about your product or service, if your copy is flat, your customers will remain unmoved. Without the 'softening' of voice tone, smiles, or friendly gestures, email sounds harsher and colder than conversation. Words you intend as humorous may come across as sarcastic and turn your readers off. TIP: Humour rarely translates well into other languages, and what's funny in one culture may be insulting in another. It's best to avoid humour altogether if your audience is international.

Writing copy

There are no hard-and-fast rules. As with every aspect of your sale, you must consider the goal and context, then choose what works best. Your prospects' time is precious so make every word count. Short and to the point is obviously preferable to long and rambling. But long copy isn't inherently bad, and in some cases it actually works better. Either way, your copy must:

- be compelling
- address benefits and not features
- succeed in overcoming the lack of nonverbal communication elements
- continually engage your readers and provide enough real value that they continue to read
- implement the AIDA principle (Attention, Interest, Desire, Action).
- follow the key steps of selling
- provide a clear call to action
- Place that call right where it needs to be in the process
- maximize the number of readers who take that action.

White papers

White papers, also known as guides or reports, may be your best chance to get the click-through you want in B2B email marketing. A free white paper or guide is still a powerful B2B offer that can stimulate high click-through rates (CTRs), capture essential company and contact information, and result in successful lead generation. According to 2001 stats compiled by eMarketer, white papers are the second most-consulted source of information by corporate end user (employee phone directories are first; market analysis is no.10). Here are some best practices for developing a white paper as a B2B marketing offer:

- In a B2B campaign, your objective is usually to generate leads. As long as you capture the qualifying contact information you need, your white paper could be about almost anything.
- A white paper should not be just black and white. If you're using it as a

marketing tool to generate leads or to brand your company as a smart-thinking one, put as much care into the look and design as you would into a print ad. In fact, think magazine layout. Use colour both in text headings and in graphics; use diagrams and flow charts. Use pull-quotes (a selected sentence or two 'pulled' from your copy and highlighted in a bigger font size). Picture your white paper printed out and lying on a decision-maker's desk. It should display your company's logo and perhaps reinforce your web site design. He or she may or may not get around to reading every word, but you will have succeeded, nonetheless, in delivering a substantive piece of product collateral.

- You want to establish yourself as credible and as an expert, but you don't want to promote your product or service too heavily. Remember the WIIFM rule, 'What's in it for me? Business users of the internet are looking for information to do their jobs. Your challenge is to convey that you feel their pain – that you understand their business need. Then, make sure the solution offered in your white paper is both broad and specific enough that the reader will learn something. A busy reader needs guidance to absorb new information. Include a background section on your industry and, at the end, a summary repeating all the key points.

- Be brief (not more than 10 to 15 pages), and make it easy to read. In addition to using colour and an eye-catching layout, deliver your key message points in bullets, and divide your copy into topics and subsections. Most of your target audience will skim and never read every word. Like an effective subject line in an email message, the title of your white paper should be a call to action or a teaser: 'Find Out How to...' or 'Top Five Mistakes...'

- The convention is to offer your white paper in Adobe's Portable Document Format (PDF). If the end user has the free version of Adobe Acrobat Reader installed on his or her computer, the file is easily downloadable and can be read anywhere, even on a personal digital assistant (PDA). You might consider including download instructions on your landing page. In any case, you should always direct your reader to the proper download page on Adobe's site (**www.adobe.com/products/acrobat/readstep2.html**). Another approach is to also include an HTML version of your white paper.

- Finally, in addition to using your white paper as an offer for an email marketing campaign, you should be promoting it from your web site, from your signature file, from an offline marketing campaign, and in any other way that gets you the leads you're looking for.

Email subject lines

We are all bombarded by email. Some of them are legitimate business correspondence; some are colleagues playing CYA ('see ya'); and some are solicitations, personal mail, junk mail, jokes or spam. With all of that clutter in your prospect's inbox, how do you give your email communication a chance of being read? There's only one way – write a great subject line following these 5 tips:

- Your prospects are always interested in one thing: What's in it for me? Write with that in mind – which means write about the benefits that matter to them, not features that matter to you. Remember that your first sale in the email communication is making them spend their valuable time reading your solicitation. If you can't write a subject line that makes them do that, what makes you think you can make them spend their money?
- Kiss them. **Keep It Short and Simple.** Write your subject line so that there are fewer than 10 words; fewer than 5 are even better.
- Don't use exclamation points at the end of the subject line. Rarely do you see personal emails that need that kind of 'noise' to grab your attention. Good business writing never does it. It doesn't need to.
- While it's generally a good thing to use the word 'you' in persuasive copy, it's a spam predictor in subject lines. Few people use the word 'you' in emails to colleagues; spam uses it frequently. The closer your subject line comes to the tone of ordinary email, the more likely it is that your message will be opened.
- Do use question marks, if doing so makes sense. Questions are much more engaging than statements. Wouldn't you agree?

Incentives

eMarketer published a report recently discussing trends and forecasts for email marketing. The study indicates that the average email user currently receives 15.2 emails daily and will receive over 20 by 2003. The study also estimates that the average recipient's 1.8 permission-based daily email (2000) will grow to 4.4 by 2003. Clearly, email clutter has become an issue, and response rates on low-quality mailings continue to decline, especially when the source is unknown. But incentives can still play an important role in acquiring qualified permission-based registrations. So use use your registration form to filter out less-qualified users. Regarding the actual incentive being used, it is important to remember that you do not have to award huge incentives to succeed. However, you should use the incentive as a second screen for filtering unqualified registrations. Make sure that the incentive is relevant to what you ultimate offer. Offering merchandise, service, or value-added upgrades for the services you sell:

- will help familiarise users with your company, its products, and services

- will help develop brand familiarity with a real user experience

- will filter out people who have no use for your service

A cash incentive is the best way to attract unresponsive contest seekers to a database, reducing the overall responsiveness of your group. Double opt-in lists will have a higher level of quality than opt-out lists, and building relationships with customers will win you business in the long run. If a user cannot remember registering, then messages received are coming from unsolicited sources in the eyes of the consumer.

Personalisation

In today's wired world, email has become an accepted form of communication, advertising and marketing. Opt-in email campaigns are pulling in higher clickthrough rates and reaping greater success than banner ads and traditional direct marketing. Why? Personalisation. First, allowing customers to opt-in is vital. Companies want to avoid spam, and empowering consumers to choose what kind of information they receive will in turn lead to higher clickthroughs, since these consumers are more likely to respond to information they specifically requested. Once companies have received permission, they must then build and implement a strict policy outlining consumers' privacy and maintain open lines of communication with the customer in regards to captured information. Consumers will continue to visit only those companies they trust and, in an internet world growing more and more crowded with new businesses, only companies that establish solid relationships with their customers will survive and thrive. Customers can experience information overload. Therefore, a greater degree of personalisation is required. The most successful companies accomplish this by allowing consumers to drill down into the specific type of information they want to receive – products, topics, even price-points. This issue of personalisation revolves around three key concepts:

Information   Gather information regarding customer habits and interests. Ask the customer directly and utilise demographics and transaction patterns to develop core value sets about the customer.

Customer interests Give customers what they want and only when they want it. Determine via direct response or captured data what kind of products customers might purchase or what type of information is most appealing to them.

Delivery   Learn how best to contact customers and what type of information they're capable of receiving. Find out how often they want to receive this information and always allow them to change their profile at any time.

Personalisation is a logical and vital piece of the email marketing puzzle. Therefore, companies must decide how best to apply the principles of personalisation to their communication with customers. Consumers want to feel that a company is catering to their specific needs, and one-to-one, personalised email marketing is the ideal means to this end. Once companies can gain permission from the consumer, develop tailored content for those customers and learn to maximise their results, email marketing will truly become the most valuable tool for businesses to maximise customer retention and value.

> Get a Hotmail (**www.hotmail.com**) account and sign up for a few of those risqué opt-in lists you've been staying away from. Watch how your inbox fills up with spam. Then take special note of the words that are common in those subject lines e.g. guarantee, debt, free, sex, easy, discount, specials and cash. These are words that people are beginning to filter out of the inbox and directly into their recycling bins. If nothing else, having a Hotmail account gives you the ability, as a marketer, to opt in to all kinds of lists and see what is happening out there in the email world while protecting your work and home email addresses - not to mention being able to access the Hotmail account from anywhere in the world.

Using autoresponders

You may associate the term autoresponders with the automated, predefined text replies that verify your opt-in or double-opt-in permission to receive email messages. But there's more to autoresponders than acknowledging your sign-up for an ezine. In fact, a number of small-business sites are using autoresponders as a powerful email marketing tactic. In contrast to downloadable PDF files, autoresponders can deliver a sequence of messages that build on one another and push the benefits of your product or service to prospective customers, rather than pulling customers to the benefits.

An autoresponder is a special e-mail address that works along the line of fax-back services. When somebody requires more information about something on your site, or in a classified ad you've placed in a newspaper or a letter you've sent them, they just need to send an e-mail to the relevant address and they instantly get back a reply providing more information. The potential client does not have to pay postage and wait for the enquiry to be acted on and returned, or pay for the cost of a phone call for a recorded message, and is therefore much more likely to respond to your offer. Additionally you are saving the costs of sending out expensive literature to people who may not be interested.

Some web hosting services now supply autoresponders with their package, but these will be linked to the server and may not be transferable if you wish to move companies. You may also be paying extra for these. The best option is to purchase independent autoresponders that you can use with, or without, any website. There are several companies that will rent you an autoresponder at a monthly fee but there are two practical alternatives:

- pay a one off fee for a single autoresponder which is yours for life
- pay an annual fee for an unlimited number of autoresponders.

If you have only one product to sell then you will only need one autoresponder and will be better off buying the single autoresponder for a one-off fee. You can also use an automated system to send follow up messages at no extra cost. If you have several products or services you may want one for each, and an annual fee for unlimited autoresponders may be more appropriate.

How might you use your autoresponders?

We received your message

Every technical support website has an autoresponder set up to notify people that they have received their email and in what time frame they can expect a response. They have discovered that people want an instant response to their email, and sending them an automatic response helps. Do you have a similar autoresponder message for your customer service or technical support address? Doing so could increase your customer satisfaction, especially if you include resources on your website where visitors may be able to find the answer to their question, such as Frequently Asked Questions pages or bulletin boards.

More information

You can encourage your visitors to email specific addresses or fill out forms forwarding to specific addresses for more information on your company, prices, etc.

Email fax-on-demand

Set up your Frequently Asked Question reports as auto response messages. This way, visitors don't have to wade through irrelevant information to find the answer to their question, and you get to collect their email addresses.

Email us for your free report

Free reports are a great marketing opportunity to encourage readers to buy your product while still making them feel like they received valuable information. You can set up a form on your website to email your autoresponder and send visitors your report via email. Benefits include weeding out bad email addresses before they get into your database, having the report sent immediately, automatically and giving you the option of promoting the autoresponder address in ezines and discussion lists where many people prefer to respond to ads via email.

Follow-up

Not all autoresponders are one-time deals. You can find 'delayed autoresponders' that allow you to set up a follow-up sequence. The most popular way to use this is to send a free report, then three to six auto response messages to encourage readers to buy your other products. Your response should improve with each sales letter you send.

Free email courses

Delayed autoresponders also give you the opportunity to create a series of free reports on a subject and send them out in sequence.

If your website host offers free autoresponders, refer to their online manual or contact their technical support for instructions on how to set up your own autoresponders. If you are working with an email program, refer to the manual. Autoresponders are easy to set up. However you choose to use your autoresponders, be sure you always check the email sent to them. Somebody might just send an important message to the wrong address. Also, don't neglect adding the email addresses you receive to your database! The people who request information from you are great prospects.

Add TouchScape's email marketing capability to your website

Click **www.touchscape.com/clkz** to view a self-guided tour of the email marketing solution that received a 4-star rating from PC Magazine. You can:

- capture visitors to your website and build your own marketing database

- segment your database by interest lists, demographics and behaviour

- launch online database marketing campaigns

- track, analyse and report on results

- monitor click-through activity

Email lists

The direct marketing industry has developed targeted e-mail lists you can rent consisting of people who have agreed to receive commercial e-mail messages. Do a smaller test first to determine the quality of the list.

List brokering
Ways a list broker can cheat an unsuspecting email marketer include:

- Dishonest list brokers send your email out to a bunch of people who have no idea how they got on the list, never mind why they might be targeted by a company such as yours. The low response rate results from poor targeting.
- In the most outright type of fraud, the brokers just didn't send many

emails out at all, aside from, perhaps, to themselves. They then respond to the offer themselves to give the semblance that some sort of response was going through, validating their claim of performance.

If the contract had a 'right to audit' clause, you would have the ability to get the email logs to see if the list broker had sent out the emails. Very few people insist on this, and fewer are able to actually exercise it. You could sue the company in civil court, provided that the damages reached a certain minimum threshold. To prove its innocence, the company would likely provide such log files. If it didn't have log files proving performance, you might win such a case. Although it wouldn't likely be profitable to any one marketer, it would keep the vendors more honest in the aftermath. Finally, you could tell the potentially dishonest company that its future billings would be dependent on current performance. Sometimes making future deals contingent on current performance will inspire an outfit to set things right, although if it's conducting outright fraud here, it might not be expecting or desiring future business from you.

To prevent this type of thing from happening in the future, list buyers should put themselves on the mailing lists prior to the email drop. That way, they know not only if the mail went out but also with what frequency and when. This also allows the buyer to see how easy it is to get off the list – a key determinant of targeting, because it allows the uninterested to leave. Buyers should insist on a right-to-audit clause in the contract, identifying what specific records must be made available on request. The most effective way to make sure this type of liability never occurs is to insist on performance-based media buys.

Opt-in elist rental

Good for a quick boost in sales. Visit **www.postmasterdirect.com**, a prominent opt-in list service provider.

Capturing email addresses

Your current website visitors are your best source of returning traffic. It is much easier to get somebody to come back to your website, when you already know they're interested in your content, than to convince somebody new to visit. Even if your visitors are bookmarking your website, they may forget about you and never return despite your good content and constant updates. By capturing your visitors' addresses, you can remind them to return, ask them for improvement ideas or new content they would like to see on your website. Direct email is the best way to attract traffic, and your previous visitors are most likely to give it to you! If you are unfamiliar with databases, or fear so many responses that it would take you hours to enter them all yourself, take heart! There are many new software programs and services out there to help you with the onerous task, and many of them are free like Listbot. They'll add a little advertisement to the bottom of your email, and you won't be able to format your email with HTML, but they'll do all the work for you, including adding new subscribers, taking people off the list who unsubscribe, and dealing with bounced and automatic response email.

If your web server supports cgi scripts, there are a number of email management scripts available for free. Setting it up could be a little work, especially if you are unfamiliar with cgi scripts, but the effort will be worth it: you'll have a new skill you can apply to adding interactivity all over your website. These scripts usually won't allow you to format your email with HTML, but they give you more control over your email than free services and won't add any advertisements. If your server doesn't support cgi scripts, or you want to use your old email program to send your emails or ezines, there are some software programs out there that can help. You can get a mail merge email program for free, or try Swiss Army App, which includes the function. You can also try something like AWeber's autoresponders, which send preset email to people in your database on the dates (or after the time period) you specify. AWeber will also keep a list of all the email addresses of people who emailed you, so you can send them a message manually, too.

On your website's response form, include a checkbox where the visitor can give you permission to e-mail updates about products or services. Capture first and last name in separate fields so you can market personally to them. But only ask for the information you need or they won't fill it out.

Using email for marketing

A feedback form allows your visitor to tell you what they think about your website, your products or services, or ask you questions. Be sure to respond when visitors ask you questions, and it's a good idea to send a thank-you note if they send you a compliment or comment.

What do you do with the addresses you've got? Send email when you have new content, products or services to offer which may interest visitors in the form of an announcement or personal message. Start an ezine and include your website address and a reason to visit or buy your product in each issue – along with valuable articles.

If you want to gather email addresses (without collecting them through advertising or your website), the only way to do it ethically is to use an opt-in mail service like YesMail. You might consider advertising in email ezines instead. Some ezines even offer 'Solo Ads' sent to subscribers without an accompanying ezine. You can also participate in newsgroups, discussion lists and bulletin boards for free and use the addresses someone else has collected. A more exciting option is to work out a deal with another business with the same target market. If they have a list of email addresses, you might be able to trade them a prize for their contest, a special deal for their customers, or a financial cut of your profits in exchange for a mailing

Closed-loop marketing

More and more sites are asking for postal addresses in addition to email addresses. A combined email/direct mail list is a potent tool that marketers can rent. It facilitates the deployment of 'closed-loop' marketing programs, whereby prospects and customers can be reached by both direct mail and email. In a closed-loop-marketing program, the direct mail piece performs the initial groundwork. It helps promote your brand, provides details on your offer, and directs prospects to your web site for more information or to place an order. Because of their relative low cost, large-format postcards have been very popular recently. An increasing number of companies in the internet marketing space are using traditional direct mail packages, including a variety of components in the envelope, e.g. brochure. The direct mail piece provides several marketing advantages. With the proper design, it can have a prolonged shelf life. This is typical with catalogues, pocket references, colour brochures, and functional items, e.g. sliding reference cards. The direct mail piece also provides an alternative response channel. It makes good business sense to allow a prospect to place an order at every point of communication.

After the direct mail piece is sent, a follow-up email can facilitate the sales conversion process and lift the response rates. You can choose to further enhance the direct mail offer with a more aggressive price point, or direct interaction via the web. The landing page that is referenced in the follow-up email should do the following:

- provide added information on your product or service

- promote the submission of information, e.g. via an offer of a PalmPilot drawing, so that subsequent conversion efforts can be made
- allow the placement of an order.

Closed-loop campaigns should also be used for your own house-list mailings. If you are collecting email addresses only from customers and prospects, you are missing out on the benefits of having the ability to send highly integrated marketing messages to those in your house list. An excellent example of a marketer collecting and renting a combined email/direct mail list is Thomas Register (**www.thomasregister.com**). It benefits from the ability to target direct mail and email campaigns at those in its combined house list. It also benefits from enhanced revenue opportunities with third-party advertisers by offering a combined email and postal list for rental. Via the 'Free Membership' link on the Thomas Register site, you can view the type of information it is collecting in exchange for free access to an online version of the Thomas Register of American Manufacturers. Notice the check boxes that allow the user to control receipt of email, both from Thomas and from third-party advertisers. Also note the privacy-policy links, which lead to a page that provides clear and concise information on how the collected data will be used.

Using digital signatures

Signatures attached to end of email messages are like business cards and should be part of every email sent out by your business. Customers and prospects will see your signature file again and again, which will only help to keep you in the minds of the recipients. You will need to decide if you want a standardised signature for everyone in the business to follow, or if you will allow everyone to be creative and come up with their own, within some guidelines of course.

A signature can spread the word about your website without any effort on your part, because it is automatically sent to everyone you send email to and is added every time you post to a newsgroup. It is nice to have an email program, which allows you to create several different signature files, so you can send different messages to different groups of people, or on different occasions. If that isn't possible, you can use different email programs depending on your situation, or just keep your signature simple. There are just a few things to remember about signature files:

Length: A signature file should be short – no longer than six lines. This is especially true for newsgroups and discussion lists, where people are receiving a lot of messages and are likely to be annoyed by excessive sales pitches.

Width: It should be no more than 60-70 characters wide, as some email systems will cut off any line longer than 80 characters and some even less.

Content: Your business name, your name, email address, other contact details; such as your phone and fax number, postal address, and what you do. Your full URL will almost always show up as a link in the recipient's email program, as long as there is no punctuation directly afterward.

Message: A short message about your company, product or service you offer. Sound and graphics files are fine, but not everyone's email program supports them. If your email takes a long time to download, or worse, you crash your prospect's computer, you will only lose business. Your signature should match the personality of your business and website. If you are a solicitor don't put cute ASCII graphics in your signature. But if you're a graphic artist, an ASCII graphic would be a wonderful idea.

Here are instructions for creating your signature on three popular programs:

Outlook Express Type up your signature file in Notepad, then open Outlook Express and choose Options from the Tools menu. Click on the Signature tab. Click the New button for the Signatures box and copy your signature from Notepad. Paste it into the Edit Signature box. Or save your signature in Notepad and click the File radio button, then Browse for your signature file.

Eudora Pro Look in your menus for Signature Files. Use the Normal template first. You can create as many signature files as you like. To send a signature other than your default, open the Signature panel on the left. You have to click one of the tabs on the bottom left of the screen, under your email boxes. Just highlight the signature you want to use and click Send.

Netscape Create a text file named 'signature.txt' or similar. Visit the Mail and News Preferences under the Options menu, and type in where your signature file is located. You can just edit the file when you want to change it.

Altavista's free IName web-based email program makes it easy to make signature files and use different ones for each email. When you write an email, there's a button next to your signature drop-menu, which allows you to create a new file. Once you've created one (or more), use the drop-menu to choose the signature file you wish to use.

Using your email addresses

Using a range of email addresses to market different divisions of your business is a good idea to convey an impression of solidarity and organisation. Commonly advertised email addresses, which you should advertise on your website for visitors to make contact with the company include:

- sales@yourdomain.com   for sales enquiries
- info@yourdomain.com   for requests of information
- help@yourdomain.com   for general enquiries
- comments@yourdomain.com   for visitors to send comments and suggestions about your website
- webmaster@yourdomain.com   for visitors to send reports of bugs, missing links, etc.
- md@yourdomain.com   for visitors who would like to contact the Chair or MD of the company

---

Hewlett-Packard sending emails in Asia

Hewlett-Packard has been using online direct marketing company Digital Impact to distribute e-mail marketing campaigns in the Chinese, Japanese and Korean markets. The goal of the campaigns was to enable Hewlett-Packard to send targeted e-mails in Asian languages to its global customer base in order to drive sales, increase web site traffic and build customer loyalty. The campaigns, which were sent to IT professionals, managers and strategists, included informational monthly updates about new site features, promotions and reminders of online strategic planning, support, training and discussion group services. Digital Impact says the e-mailings resulted in double-digit open and click-through rates. Since it began tailoring its monthly e-mail newsletter to Asia-Pacific customers with messages in their native languages, Hewlett-Packard's IT Resource Center has seen click-through rates double.

Direct email

Sending announcements of your new website or a major change in your existing website to potential and current clients is a good idea. The trick is to sell them your website by telling them how they will benefit by visiting. When sending promotional email, make certain the recipients will be interested in your message. If you are accused of spamming, your ISP and website host may discontinue your service. You can make sure by either using a list of email addresses culled from responses to your website or by buying a list of people who have expressed interest in your type of product or service. If you don't already collect the addresses of your website visitors, start now so you can encourage them to return through email.

Targeted mailing

The internet offers thousands of very targeted mailing lists and news groups made up of people with very specialised interests. Use DejaNews **www.dejanews.com** to find appropriate sources. Don't bother with news groups constituted of 'spam.' Instead, find groups where a dialog is taking place. Don't use aggressive marketing and overtly plug your product or service. Rather, add to the discussion in a helpful way and let the signature at the end of your e-mail message do your marketing for you. People will gradually get to know and trust you, visit your site, and do business with you.

> Offering something for free, like a report, ezine, or sample, will get you more email addresses than feedback forms and guestbooks. If you don't mind offering something bigger, like a larger product or complete service, start a contest. If you market to webmasters, consider offering a website award program or a free ad on your website.

Marketing to your house list

E-mail regularly to your growing house list of site visitors and customers – but not too often, otherwise recipients will feel you're abusing the limited permission they've granted you. But once or twice a month is necessary to keep your company in the forefront of your recipients' consciousness. Marketing is best done in conjunction with useful information that interests your visitors. That's why sending a brief ezine not only informs, but also builds your brand and customer trust, as well as providing the context for offers of your products and services. Remember, you'll probably get only a single chance to capture a website visitor's e-mail address. But if you can obtain an e-mail address and permission, you'll be able to inexpensively market to that visitor again and again for the life of the e-mail address and make sales that eluded you on a customer's first visit. E-mail marketing to your house list is an essential strategy. Once you get visitors to your website, your next important task is to secure their e-mail address and their permission to e-mail them your ezine, occasional updates, or new product or service information.

Referrals

Include a link on your website, which allows visitors to recommend it to a friend. These emails are the best source of traffic you could possibly get! They contain glowing testimonials by people potential visitors know urging them to visit your website, and you don't have to do anything.

Selling to your existing customer base

By taking the database that companies already own and manage – that is, opt-in/permission-based lists – businesses have an opportunity to upsell to their existing customers, an easier and more cost-effective process than obtaining a new customer. The true potential of email marketing lies in targeting specific products and services to your existing customer base, consumers who already know your company and, hopefully, know the value of your products and services. Each email delivered to your customer base should be treated as an opportunity to inform customers about promotions, specials, or new products – and increase your revenue. You already have their loyalty, and this certainly makes them receptive to your message.

Targeting your existing customer base is a great way to build your company's web presence. At the same time, it's an excellent opportunity to make your current customer base aware of other value-added services your company provides, such as expert advice, community chat rooms, or free samples. If you want to sell more products quickly and efficiently, look at creating an opt-in email list for your existing customer base and begin marketing new products and services to them.

SPAM

Spamming is sending unsolicited email. Sending a message to someone you have never met, nor had a prior business relationship with, who did not give you their email address and certainly never asked you to send them anything is unethical and, in many cases, illegal. If your ISP or website host receives even a few complaints that you have sent Spam, they may revoke your service – possibly without giving you a chance to defend yourself. This makes sending any kind of large-scale mailing risky, including opt-in ezines.

A recent study by FloNetwork (**www.flonetwork.com**) indicated that 31 percent of online consumers would like to receive permission-based email once per week. Another 12 percent would like to receive such emails on a daily basis, while 18 percent would like them a couple of times per week.

Make sure visitors to your site know what's going to happen. Have a separate form for them to fill out, or in the case of an autoresponder, make them send a blank email. On all your website's forms, you could include a little checkbox giving visitors the chance to subscribe to your ezine or promotional email sequence. If you want more people to subscribe and aren't as worried about upsetting people, include a check box subscribing them, allowing them to uncheck the box if they don't want more email. You have a website, but no opt-in list of email addresses.

There are 5 levels when it comes to sending people 'invitations' to visit your website.

Level 1: Sending colleagues, and previous customers non-sales messages. Sending other business owners or their representatives invitations to swap ads or otherwise help each other get more traffic and/or sales. Sending double-opt-in email ezines and specifically requested sales information.

Level 2: Emailing colleagues, and previous customers invitations and sales messages without asking. Also, sending 'follow-up' email automatically for purchases and/or freebie requests or using a double-opt in email address list (such as YesMail).

Level 3: Forcing people to fill out a form to receive a freebie and automatically signing them up for your newsletter, using a list of email addresses received through a professional association you belong to, and in any other way collecting email addresses to send people sales messages (except actual customers) without letting them know what they're getting themselves into.

Level 4: Collecting email addresses on your website through a guest book, free for all link page, or bulletin board and sending them a sales message for your product or service without warning can get people steamed up. Visiting websites and emailing the webmaster or replying to email messages sent to you with your sales message is a Level 4.

Level 5: Gathering email addresses off websites or newsgroups by using a 'bot' or spider and sending the people on the list a sales message for your product or service is unethical and will probably result in some nasty repercussions. Buying a cheap list of email addresses is really just paying someone else to do this for you.

Level 1 is always okay. Level 2 is okay under most circumstances. Level 3 is probably okay on a small scale. Level 4 is something to stay away from, but if you can gather snail mail addresses instead, it is okay to send the people sales messages that way. Never, under any circumstances, use Level 5.

If you plan to gather a large list of email addresses for your business, protect yourself from malicious subscribers. Be sure to get everyone's permission to send them email and keep it. Choose a regional ISP and talk to them personally about what you are doing, so they know you are honest and ethical and will contact you before taking action if they receive complaints. To ethically use a large list, you either have to gather it yourself or buy it from an ethical company – which will not be cheap. Here are some suggestions:

1. Build a great website that will appeal to search engines and submit it to the top ones by hand.
2. Read as many marketing articles as possible for more ideas.
3. Post non-sales messages to related topics on bulletin boards, newsgroups, and discussion lists. Include a signature file containing a benefit-laden headline, response email and a URL.
4. Email your colleagues to invite them to your website and ask them to spread the word to their own colleagues.
5. Advertise your website offline too.

Setting up a preference page

Customers should be telling you their preferences directly, e.g. how often they want to receive content and offers. Customer acceptance is determined by how interested customers are in the marketer's value proposition, so you need to ask questions in order to gauge that interest. A problem that goes hand-in-hand with the frequency problem is the notion of acceptance of plain text, HTML, and rich media email. Marketers can effectively kill two birds with one stone by setting up a preference page that allows permission email subscribers to set both frequency and format preferences on the same form.

Giving good email service

Good customer service is a vital aspect of any company's business. When done properly, it creates unparalleled loyalty. Companies can save time and money using e-mail as a customer relationship management (CRM) tool and consumers often prefer it. Opportunities for customer relationship e-mail include:

ezines	newsflashes
new product or service announcements	new product availability
promotional discount offers	referral/viral marketing
traditional direct marketing campaigns	transactions
order confirmations	personalised thank you messages
shipping status	bill fulfilment
customer service marketing	customer surveys
reminders (replenishment notification)	alerts
expiration notices	change of service notifications
technical support for products and services	

In the future, e-mail, especially customer service communications, will play a bigger role in CRM. A 2001 AMR Research study found that e-mail is one of the top CRM deployments. A recent study found that most consumers expect to get a response to their e-mail inquiry within six hours. Unfortunately, only 38% of companies are providing that kind of speedy service and 33% are taking three days or longer to respond. Even worse, 24% of companies do not respond to e-mail inquiries at all.

Your e-mail message should be designed to get people to visit your web site, not sell them your product or service. To do that, the best approach is to offer them something free, e.g. a newsletter, and make it easy to sign up. That way, you don't lose those who visit but don't buy. Keep your e-mail message short, stimulate their interest and curiosity, emphasise the value of the free material awaiting them, and offer them a sample of what you're giving away. For example, your invitation might just be four or five lines, designed to stimulate key motivations and then promising to satisfy them by a visit to your site. For example, if you sell home decorations, your e-mail might ask the question, 'Do you know how to give your entire home a brand new look for less than most people pay for a kitchen? We do! Visit us at www.wearecheap.com to learn more. And get a free home analysis and hundreds of free tips on making your home a showplace your friends will envy. I've included a few of those tips below.' Probably the most important tip is to write several different letters and test them out on small parts of your list. See which ones get the best response, and use them. Once you're getting a good return, see if you can expand into other regions, countries, or related interest groups.

Email marketing plan optimisation

Ask yourself these review questions prior to each email campaign:

- Who are my customers, and what do they need?
- What is the solution that I'm offering to my customers? Often, products are released under the guise of a solution when they're really not solving any real customer problem. Consider not only what you believe your product or service to be but also how your customers perceive it. Also, how is your solution different from the one your competitors are touting? Make sure your customers understand the benefits of your solution and how it's different from others out there.
- How am I communicating this solution to my customers? Communicating at the right pitch and frequency to a target audience,

with a message that the audience perceives as valuable, should be a cornerstone of every marketing plan. To maximize the brand impact, and ultimately a campaign's return on investment, work hard to ensure that your various customer touch points present an integrated brand message and personality.

- What is the purpose of this specific campaign? For example, during the planning stages of your marketing plan, you may state that you will, among other tactics, execute two email campaigns per month during the year. In addition to having a specific purpose for every tactic within a marketing plan, you should also include learning objectives. What do you want to learn about your customers from this campaign? What bits of data – demographic, behavioural, or other – can you capture that will help you be more effective the next time you're planning tactics?

- What metrics will I use to gauge the campaign's effectiveness? Goals are valuable only when they are measured.

- What will I do if the campaign shows signs of being ineffective? Always have an alternate plan that is well thought out, in case the first set of tactics doesn't seem to be working. Upfront market research and focus groups might offer a lot of insight into what tactics will deliver the greatest return, but the true test doesn't come until the market reacts.

Buy a text ad in an email newsletter

Businesses are finding that some of the best advertising buys are for small 4 to 12 line ads in established e-mail newsletters. Ads can both inform and motivate readers to click on the URL, and tend to bring much more targeted visitors.

---

4 TIPS!

☒ Use your desktop email client to broadcast your messages

Use of a desktop client to send your marketing message seems like a very logical choice when your list is small and you are sending only text but either of the following may occur as a result:

- Any mail you send from your desktop client is going to affect your corporate network, and depending on volume and message size you could be creating email problems for your entire company. Between outgoing messages and incoming replies, you will affect the load on the servers. Check with your IT contact if you are sending email this way and include it in those decisions you are making about your email marketing efforts.

● There is an increasing number of articles in the internet news about email messages that mistakenly get sent in such a way that the entire list of addresses is exposed or that subscribers' replies or 'unsubscribe me' messages go to the entire list. Suffice it to say there is no better way to 'burn' your list than to expose it to spammers and clog up subscribers' mailboxes.

☒ Don't risk your corporate domain

The ISPs are getting more sophisticated about determining spam versus wanted email. For years, they have been trashing mail that is perceived to be spam, and you may never know that your mail was not received. This applies not only to your marketing messages but also to any of your company's email. The major email service providers work with the ISPs to get 'white hat' domain names that will ensure that mail coming from those domains will be delivered.

☒ Always include the unsubscribe/remove link

Make sure that your recipients know that you are watching out for them. Use language such as 'if you no longer wish to receive,' or 'If you believe you've received this in error – .' And make sure that your unsubscribe link works.

☒ Always remind the recipients who you are and how you know them

Every email message you send should remind the recipient of who you are and how they came to be on your email list. Who you are can be in the 'From' line, or you can actually state it in your opening. Your text or HTML messages should have an introductory statement that briefly says, 'You are receiving this because – '

Reviewing your email communications

Email marketing should help you drive traffic to your web site to build your business. The results can have multiple benefits: list rental to find new customers, sponsorships of others' email, efforts to capture leads and to communicate with your interested audiences, and so on. Here are some tips on reviewing your email communications to ensure you're getting responses that yield sales:

Is your call to action clear? Be clear about where the link is taking them e.g. Click here to enter our contest. Believe it or not, it's not always clear, and, due to browser and mail client inconsistencies, you need to make sure readers know how to get to what you are offering.

Can readers forward to a friend? Viral or referral marketing is the best way to build your list. We all tell our friends about good service experiences, something nice someone has done for you, an offer that is too good to pass up. Get your audience to spread the word. Again, you need to be clear and bold about asking for readers' help. Put the mention in every communication. Consider creating a campaign that rewards people who forward and actually create new additions to your list. It can be done manually, but it is much easier when using email solution providers that have options to help you track forwarded mail. Best-of-breed providers allow you to track individuals who actually forwarded the message, and then also track the conversions from those forwarded messages. If you are managing a smaller list, manually creating a reward campaign can be done by setting up a mailbox that lets people send you a note that says, 'Fred Bloggs, email@address, referred me to your list.' Once you get three like that for Fred, reward him. You can reinforce the entire campaign in your email by letting people know who is referring and how much and what they have received in return for their hard work.

Sponsorships and ads. If your email or web site's existence relies on traffic or on click-throughs for advertisers, make sure you remind your audience to patronise your sponsors. Choosing advertisers and sponsors relevant to the content will greatly improve the responses from your recipients. Your audience may need that reminder, especially when you are advertising your own services or products.

Are you tracking your links? Even if you are not using a sophisticated email broadcasting solution that provides click-through data, you can isolate pages on your site by looking closely at your log files. This takes coordination among the people managing your web server, your webmaster and you. When your webmaster creates a page for you, make sure that your log-file reporting will provide you information about how many impressions are served off the page that 'called the action' in your email message.

6

Marketing Using Ezines

CLICK-ONS

Why an ezine?

Building customer relations

Starting an ezine

Creating content

HTML and ezines

Gathering email addresses for your ezine

Linking

Ezine distribution

Why an ezine?

What's the best way to get your customers and interested web surfers to remember you and your product or service? Sign them up for your company's ezine (electronic newsletter). If you haven't started an ezine yet, here are five reasons you should:

Open a pipeline of influence   If you remain an independent source of knowledge and information – resisting the temptation to bombard your subscribers with ads and promotions – readers will be more receptive to your messages about your products and services.

Attract new customers

If your e-mail list is a success, subscribers will forward your messages to friends and colleagues, who might subscribe and click through to your site.

Prevent customer loss

The best trail that a potential customer can leave is an e-mail address. Once you have that address, you have the chance to remind that person regularly of your company and products or services. But make sure that your e-mail messages provide useful information. And if some message topics don't specifically promote your company, be creative. Find ways to work in your company name and what you sell.

Keep yourself on your toes

Managing an e-mail list forces you constantly to consider your business's current market position. Assigning yourself publication deadlines for your e-mail list pushes you to fine-tune your marketing strategies.

Promote your credibility

E-mail lists are a great way to show you care about customers and are confident enough to share what you've learned. By providing relatively unbiased and reliable information, you build credibility. Subscribers will associate the quality of the information you provide with the quality of your products and services.

Set objectives

What do you want the ezine to accomplish? Inform your customers and prospects of new products or services? Serve as a value-added source of technical information? Help your customers more effectively use your products or services?

Take heed of these five golden rules of e-mail marketing:

1. Don't make promises you can't keep

It's easy to underestimate the time it takes to write an ezine. Don't overestimate your ability to deliver frequent, regular publications. You want to promote reliability and quality; this can't be done on empty promises.

2. Provide useful content

An ezine that doesn't contribute anything to its subscribers' knowledge base is useless to them and harms your company's reputation. To determine which topics your ezine should cover, think of information that speaks to the needs of your audience.

3. Do not send unsolicited e-mail messages

Only subscribers should receive mailings. Do not include e-mail addresses from your personal address book or those gathered from business cards or other sites or those bought from e-mail address providers. Start by drawing on your database of e-mail addresses from customers who have expressed interest in receiving more information from you. Send an introductory message, giving them the option to subscribe or decline subsequent mailings. As a courtesy, send an e-mail confirmation back to new subscribers to make sure the owner of the e-mail address really is interested in your ezine.

4. Provide easy unsubscribing

Unsubscribing must be as easy as subscribing. If unsubscribe directions aren't clearly posted along with instructions for subscribing, customers might be reluctant to sign up. Even more, you don't want current subscribers to feel trapped.

5. Respond to feedback

Don't be afraid to make minor adjustments to your list in response to subscriber feedback and be sure to communicate these changes to subscribers in advance.

While it's a big commitment in time, publishing a weekly, monthly, or quarterly ezine is one of the best ways to keep in touch with your prospects, generate trust, develop brand awareness, and build future business. You can distribute your ezine using your e-mail program, or have people subscribe on your website directly to a listserver program (such as Majordomo) offered by your ISP.

Building customer relations

Many business owners have found having an ezine is a valuable tool in building relationships with their customers and prospective customers. The ezine must have a personal communication from a focal person in the business. To the customer, this person is the business. For a small business, this is usually the business owner. The messages should be 'I' messages, not 'We' messages. The messages don't have to be technical. They can be 'gossip.' Did company employees participate in a fundraiser or a community service project? That regular personal message is the most important part of the ezine, and should be the first item of the ezine. Customers or prospective customers should eventually feel they are receiving a personal letter from a friend. Your ezine should also include other information your customers or prospective customers will want to read. What are the new developments relating to your business? Are you offering new products or services? How are other customers benefiting from your product or service?

Website ezines	These are basically a web site with text, graphics and audio. Some web ezines or newsletter are free while others charge a subscription fee.
Email ezines	These are delivered directly to your email address and are mostly free subscriptions. They are text only. This is an excellent way to advertise directly to your target audience.

Starting an ezine

Ezines are a relatively new phenomenon, and starting one can bring new business and help you keep customers longer, but there are no hard and fast rules or statistics to measure yourself against. Be creative with your content and promotion, and the subscribers will trickle in. It doesn't hurt to offer some sort of incentive, like free ads to subscribers, an ebook, or a screen saver.

> How often should you issue the ezine? If you're not contacting your customers at least every three months, they're probably forgetting you. Monthly is much better. More frequent contact helps to keep you on the front of your customers' minds and helps make them more resistant to your competitors.

Short ezines are great. People can read them in the email program in a reasonable amount of time and are more likely to click on your links. The more often you send your ezine, the shorter it should be. 1-3 pages is best for daily ezines, and 10-15 pages seem to be typical for monthly ezines with weeklies falling anywhere in between.

If you have a daily ezine, an article or a tip a day is all you need to worry about. If you're sending your ezine weekly or monthly, you may want to have a regular column or two to go along with your feature article. The best columns have a regular theme. If your website is selling something, people will be more likely to trust you and buy from you if they hear from you once a week or once a month.

> If your website sells advertisement space, ezine ads present a higher value to advertisers (than banner ads) and can increase your revenue.

Be prepared to –

- Spend time supporting your ezine by emailing subscribers personally. There will always be some people who have difficulty getting subscribed or 'unsubscribed,' or have questions.
- Be punctual. Subscribers notice when your ezine reaches them the same day every week, or the same day every month. Pick a time or day of the week or month to send it out, and make an effort to be on time. A regular, reliable publication is a sign of professionalism, and people will trust the information in your newsletter and on your website more. They will also be more likely to buy from you!
- Promote your ezine. A link from your website is probably not enough. Consider this indirect marketing for your website. Everyone who subscribes to your ezine will probably visit your website more than once, and some people just considering subscribing will visit your website.

To lighten your creative load, consider asking someone else to write a column for your ezine, publishing short guest articles, or even asking your subscribers for questions to publish with answers.

Creating content

What's the secret to launching a visually compelling, results-driven HTML ezine that will generate more qualified leads, inspire customer loyalty, reinforce your brand, lower your cost of customer acquisition and possibly deliver an incremental stream of revenue? If your ezine isn't consistently engaging, useful and relevant, you're not likely to achieve the business objectives you've set. So how do you choose the content to fill your ezine, issue after issue?

Try putting on an editor's hat while thinking like a marketer. Your best bet is to take some time to figure out what your audience is interested in. Think carefully about your product or service and what problem it solves for your target market. What is their 'pain point'? Remember, to them it's all about 'what's in it for me' (WIIFM), not about what you want to tell them.

Less is more
This is a good rule of thumb, whether for text or HTML. Use your layout to clearly package one main topic – your lead story. Then, if you have regular features or departments, run them down the left or right-hand column. Don't worry about number of words so much as the number of different articles, topics, and instant facts. Dole your information out in digestible bites. You want to leave a lasting impression, both with design/layout and with content. So concentrate on one topic per issue.

Voice and personality
This is key. If you want your ezine to develop a loyal following, it's got to have a personality, even quirkiness. Get that personality into your subject line. Use it in all your copy. Even if you're sending your ezine to hundreds or thousands, write as if it's one-to-one.

Visual appeal
Use colour, art, white space, and photographs to make your ezine visually appealing. It should stand out among all the other communications your customers receive and should be easy to read.

Reader-oriented content

Like your advertising, focus on the information needs of the reader. The ezine will be read more thoroughly, and you will gain credibility and respect.

Keep it short

Most of your readers are inundated with messages every day. No one has time to read everything. If your objectives require lengthy articles, be sure that they provide substantial reward to the reader for taking the time to read them.

Lighten up

Even the most technical ezine should give the reader a brain break with a lighter anecdote or article.

Seek contributions

Ask for input from customers, external experts and other company departments. Involvement creates commitment and support.

Prf, prof, proof

Typos and poor grammar cause breakdowns in communications and weaken company image. With a strong commitment to excellence, your marketing ezine can become one of the most effective tools in your communications arsenal.

> There are services available to provide some 'filler' material, such as clip art or cartoons.

Five Tips for Great Ezine Content

Tip 1: It's OK to repeat yourself

If one of your objectives is to stay on the mind of the prospects and customers on your subscriber list, you're more apt to succeed if your ezine has an ongoing thread. Write a series of articles that build one upon another. At the conclusion of each one, include a teaser promoting what comes next. In addition, part of repeating yourself is to use a consistent format. Whether your ezine is in text or HTML, your repeated content should include your unsubscribe instructions, your hint to pass it along to a colleague, and so forth.

Tip 2: Package your message

Use a number that lets you package your message so that it is easily digestible and lets you be a bit clever. Five tips or ten tips sounds good. I once wrote a long series of articles for a glossy business magazine entitled 'The 39 Ways to – '. Another way to package is to use factoids and snippets of information from expert sources to buttress your main topic.

Tip 3: Learn from your competition

Constantly scan other companies' or organisations' ezines to get new ideas for content, writing style, personality, voice, and so on. If you've got someone on your team with a strong stomach for email overload, get him or her to sign up for a bunch of the ezines published by internet.com (**http://.e-newsletters.internet.com**). You'll quickly be able to tell what's an effective voice and what's not.

Tip 4: Great copy is key

Copywriting for email marketing, ezines and web sites is an art. You're writing for a global audience, but you're speaking to one person at a time. How do you make your content or information 'need to know,' and how do you get your ezine to rise above the confusion of the inbox? One way to find out is to get a third party perspective. Recruit an outside copywriter and ask him or her to be ruthless when determining whether your ezine is any good.

For tips on copywriting and content, check out weekly discussion lists: I-Copywriting (**www.adventive.com/lists/icopywriting//summary.html**) and I-Content (**www.adventive.com/lists/icontent//summary.html**)

Tip 5: Plan ahead and look back

This ties in with setting a business objective for your ezine. If your goal is to convert more leads to sales, you'll need to think way ahead, at least 6 or 12 months. Make up an editorial calendar. But be ready to switch gears based on what arouses the interest of your readers. Whether text or HTML, your articles should frequently link back to pages on your web site.

There is free content for ezines available on the internet. DON'T USE IT! Don't subject your subscribers to another cookie-cutter newsletter. They deserve better and they will appreciate your effort.

Formatting ezines

Follow these directions to put simple formatting in your ezine that will give your ezine a professional appearance:

1. Use Microsoft Word document.
2. Choose Courier New type.
3. Type a single line with any character repeated 69 times.
4. Adjust margins so that this text appears in one line.
5. Press the Enter/Return key couple of times.
6. The Word document is now formatted – save as a Word document.
7. To start new document, open this file.
8. Delete the top line and set up your ezine.
9. You may use text formatting such as indents, left/centre/right/ justified, etc. These will remain intact. You may use numbering but bullets are not acceptable.
10. Design your ezine, use separators like ~~~~~, -----, and other line styles. Letters sometimes are excellent like vvvvvvv, or ^^^^^^^^^^^^^. Be creative.
11. Use white space generously. It opens up the ezine and gives ease to reading.
12. When done, save first as a Word document, then save your work as the 'Text with Layout,' or as 'MS-DOS text with Layout' file type. You then may open this file in any text-based software like e-mail software, basic text editors like Notepad, EditPad, etc. All formatting will remain intact.
13. To send the ezine, after you have opened the file in your e-mail software, just copy the text into your e-mail and send it.

Probably the number one thing you can do to keep your text ezine looking professional is use a set maximum for your line length (in characters). This is important so that your text doesn't end up looking a lot like this:

```
This is an example of a badly formatted
paragraph
where lines get chopped in the strangest of
places.
Several things can cause this. Let's take
a
look at them.
```

Why does this happen? First of all, the lines of the e-mail messages that you send may be too long, thus forcing the reader's e-mail program to push one or two words from each line onto the next one. You can get around this by using hard carriage returns ('enter' or ↵ key) at the end of 65 or so character lines. You have two options then: Either use a monospace font e.g. Courier and manually press the Enter key at the end of each line, or get yourself a text editor like TextPad (**www.textpad.com**) and set it to insert hard carriage returns at the end of each 65-character line. This is one time when a word processing program like Microsoft Word isn't the best tool to use.

Another reason that this kind of thing can happen is if you're using hard carriage returns at the end of, say, 65 character lines, but your e-mail program is only set to allow 60 character lines. Obviously, the lines will all get chopped here as well, but as you send it, before it ever reaches the reader. Make sure your e-mail preferences are set larger than your hard return line length.

Above the fold

This is another one of those buzz phrases floating around on the net these days. What it actually refers to is the first screen view when a document is opened, the portion above the fold created by the bottom of the monitor screen or application window, whichever happens to be smaller. Here's a couple of ways that being aware of this fold can help ezine publishers:

1. Include your complete web site URL in the first few lines of your ezine. When somebody opens your message, they may only give you a few seconds of their time, so putting your URL right there in front of them, above the fold, will simultaneously remind them where your message is coming from, as well as increasing your brand awareness and encouraging click-throughs. If your URL is below the fold, many of your subscribers may never see it.
2. On the first screen view of the first page of your web site, include a subscription form for your ezine. One of the most important things a site visitor can do is give you their e-mail address. If they have to go hunting for a way to do so, they may not do it at all. Put it right there in front of them: above the fold.

NOTE: Ideally, you might put a subscription form above the fold on every page of your site.

HTML and ezines

Here are some of the advantages of an HTML-format ezine over a plain-text ezine:

- You have more control over hyperlinks and other elements in your ezine. You don't have to worry about including a visible 'mailto:' before all e-mail links (although you would need this in the HTML code).
- Because your subscribers will be viewing a web page of sorts in their e-mail client, it is a much more seamless experience for them to click through to your web site. Most readers of HTML e-mail do so while connected to the internet.
- You can include pictures, graphs, graphics, colours and styled fonts in your ezine. It is more like publishing a traditional magazine or web site than a plain-text newsletter.
- You can serve interactive text or graphical ads to your subscribers, thus improving performance for your advertising clients. You'll also be able to track the actual number of impressions and click-throughs on their ad, rather than just the number of recipients.
- You will be able to judge how many of your subscribers are actually opening your ezine. This can be accomplished easily by having images pulled from the web when the message is opened.

Because many HTML ezine publishers do not include the full text of individual articles, but just a summary with a link to the full article on the web. Even if you do include full articles, HTML format makes it easier to include supplemental article summaries and links. You might also choose to include a sidebar or some other form of navigation that will allow your subscribers to easily explore some of the regions of your web site. Links to your archives, areas of an on-site directory, a 'search your site' page, your media kit, and reprint information will be useful to your subscribers. Ideally, you will offer both a text and HTML version of your ezine.

Gathering email addresses for your ezine

☑ List your ezine on one of many ezine directories on the web, such as:
- Liszt – the mailing list directory (**www.liszt.com**)
- The List of Lists (**http://catalog.com/vivian/interest-group-search.html**)
- The Flying Inkpot's Zine Scene (**http://inkpot.com/zines**)

☑ Send your ezine's description and subscription instructions to every announcement list you can find!

☑ Consider using bulk e-mail to find more people who may be interested in what you sell. You've probably heard of spam, or unsolicited e-mail advertisements. In the internet culture, it is a no-no. Instead, look for companies which offer 'opt-in' e-mail lists. These are lists of people who have indicated they would like to receive information about some topic, such as new business opportunities, health care products, etc. You will pay for each name, just like you would for a mail house list. The value is that you have a receptive audience, and you save most of the costs associated with a regular bulk mailing through the Post Office.

☑ Put your ezine subscription form on all your web pages, and give your visitors a good incentive to sign up, not just that it is free. Because free ezines are now so commonplace, 'free' no longer suffices as an incentive. Try offering a gift or a service in return for customers signing up.

☑ Use viral marketing. Post your ezine articles on the internet with instructions on how to subscribe. You can post the articles on your web site or through free content distributors on the internet, which will reach more potential subscribers. Consider these sites:
  ● Web-Source (**www.web-source.net**)
  ● List-Resources (**www.list-resources.com**)
  ● E-ZinesZ (**www.e-zinez.com**)
  ● MediaPeak.com (**www.mediapeak.com**)

☑ Purchase advertising space for your ezine in other ezines that are sent to your target audience. You can approach them directly or use an ad broker. Brokers include:
  ● MyPoints.com (**www.mypoints.com**)
  ● 24/7 (**www.sift.com**)
  ● YesMail (**www.yesmail.com**)

☑ Use ad exchanges. On an exchange, you swap ads with another ezine. This works best, of course, if the other ezine targets your audience but does not compete with your business. As long as the other ezine is directed toward your target audience, it doesn't matter if it has a large subscriber base or not; the point is that you are advertising to the people who are most likely to be interested in your ezine.

☑ Finally, you may want to: send press releases, announce it in newsgroups, mention it in discussion lists, add it to directories, add it to your signature file, put an ad in your local paper or make fliers.

Acquiring subscribers

- Have a clear objective for the ezine, e.g. to reinforce your business brand, to attract new clients or to develop a potential new source of revenue through advertising.
- Create an offer that is both compelling and related to your business's core competences.
- Ensure you have list hosting, delivery and management solutions for the opt-in list you are building.
- Work with a technically savvy web designer who also understands how an online marketing promotion works.
- If you have a limited marketing budget, negotiate for paid space in ezines and swap ads for placement in others.
- Write great copy to drive click-throughs to your web site and run your copy by a handful of tough colleagues whose opinions you respect.
- Create a landing page on your web site that is simple, seductive, and will convert a high percentage of the click-throughs to subscribers.
- Create a 'Welcome' email message in which you could include a link to the download page for your any free offers. If there's an offer, where do you access the link to the download? In an email message? On a web page? Both?
- Create a confirmation page.
- Drive sign-ups to the ezine through a sponsorship text ad.
- Tag the URLs in your sponsorship ads with unique identifiers.
- Test the sign-up process for an ezine on other sites to see how it works.
- Have sign-up boxes on every page of your web site and a Privacy Policy page. (look at other privacy policies, and crib from one you like the sound of – and don't make it too technical.)
- Promote it through your signature file and tell everyone, 'I'm launching an ezine. Be sure to sign up!'

Linking

How many links and to what? Again, there's no absolute right or wrong. The Economist (**www.economist.com**) sends out an attractive weekly ezine with a navigation bar linking back to its web site. That works because it's in the business of selling content. Maybe it's right for you because you want to promote certain areas of your site. ICONOCAST (**www.iconocast.com**), the insider-ish HTML-only ezine about internet marketing, features an

'Archives' tab at the top – good idea if you want to send readers back to previous issues on your site. The point is, think strategically about why you're using links.

Ezine distribution

You have basically 4 options when distributing your list:

Free email list hosting	There are several good free e-mail list hosting providers that will make the job of sending your ezine (and managing your list) simple. The drawback of using one of these services is that they'll advertise on your mailings. Also, because they're free, customer or technical support may be non-existent.
Using your email program	Pasting your ezine list into the BCC (Blind Carbon Copy) field is sufficient for really small lists. Be aware, however, that certain ISPs, e.g. AOL, have filters in place to trash messages with more than a certain number of addresses in the BCC field (25 or so). They do this to prevent their users from getting spammed. NOTE: Don't use CC. No one likes to see their address being broadcast all over the net.
Your own list server	This offers you the most control, but will also take the most work to set up. There are some very good list server software packages out there, some of which are free. If you're technically savvy, this may be the way to go. Many good virtual web hosting providers include support for list software.
Fee-based list hosting	This is where you pay someone to host your list. You should get good customer support and much better performance than the free hosts, but there are a lot of hack operations out there, so shop around.

9 steps to starting your own ezine:

1 First, decide how many subscribers you want to have, and what sort of people you want them to be. This will help you determine your topic, title, and how to promote your ezine. It will also help you decide how you will deliver your ezine.

2 If you plan to have just a few subscribers, it might be fine to keep your subscribers in your email program's address book and add and remove

them by hand. This gives you complete control over your subscriber list, you never miss an important email going to the wrong email box, and it requires no new software or services to implement. If you feel Netscape isn't quite up to the task, try Outlook, Eudora, or Pegasus.

3   If you are managing your subscriber list on your own, be sure your formatting works for as many email clients as possible, and your subscribers aren't receiving your whole email address list. Send a test copy to yourself and a colleague using a different email program, and a free email account.

4   For a moderate number of subscribers, you may want to try one of the free services, like ListBot (**www.listbot.com**) or set up a CGI program on your website to deal with the subscriptions. The alternative is to find a mailing list management program on the internet, e.g. Arial Software's Campaign (**www.arialsoftware.com**). If you eventually plan to have a lot of subscribers (say 10,000), you may want to hire a service to manage your list. They'll take care of everything, but it will cost.

5   Next, determine if your ezine will be daily, weekly, or monthly. Send your newsletter less often than you update your website, or there will be no reason for them to come back for a visit. Lead them back to your website each time you send an ezine by highlighting your new website content.

6   Once you have decided what, when, who, and how you are going to send your ezine, write short, medium, and long descriptions of your ezine (2 sentences, 1 paragraph, and 1 screen long).   Include subscription instructions and your website address in the medium and long descriptions.

7   Use your long description for a 'press release' you send to your clients, relevant newsgroups and ezines. Remember to include contact information in your press release.

8   Design a page of your website around your long description to sell your ezine, where visitors can subscribe. Put a link to this page on every other page of your website.

9   Finally, promote your website anywhere you can. Swap ads. Announce it on Listserv **mailto:new-list@listserv.nodak.edu** using your paragraph-long description. Put it in every ezine directory you can find. Tell people you meet. Mention it in discussion lists.

NOTE: Don't send unsolicited email or encourage anyone else to do so on behalf of your ezine.

The top seven webmaster ezines

Here are some key ezines you can subscribe to and learn from:

WebPromote Weekly
www.webpromote.com

> Weekly search engine developments by the experts. These are the same people who put out WebPosition. You'll learn something every time their newsletter comes out, because they won't send it if they don't have anything to say.

Ezine Tips
www.ezine-tips.com

> If you are planning to start your own newsletter, this ezine covers how to do it, how to promote it, and where to promote it.

List Tips
www.list-tips.com

> Tips for discussion lists and occasionally ezines, List Tips covers how to do it, how to promote it, and where to promote it. By the same publisher as Ezine Tips. Visit the entire website family at www.List-Universe.com.

Web Success Monthly
www.lrsmarketing.com

> Web Success Monthly always has great articles, plus several regular columns. Regular columns include tips, technical advice, search engine answers, and website reviews. Several authors are involved, making for a variety of valuable information.

Website Tribune
www.webmaster-resources.com/tribune

> This weekly ezine always includes a feature article and a website marketing or design tip, plus a cgi script or free software recommendation. The articles and tips are always helpful and original, but you can read it just for the script or software recommendation.

Web Marketing Today
www.wilsonweb.com

> This is serious stuff. A monthly ezine packed with original articles. There is also a monthly link list highlighting other articles of interest.

Virtual Promote Gazette
http://virtualpromote.com

> Good articles and free tools.

7

16 Exciting Marketing Ideas

CLICK-ONS

Delivering an autoresponder minicourse
Multilevel membership programs
Using seminars to generate leads
Freebie marketing ploys
Running a contest
Writing articles
Banners
Affiliate programmes
Paid advertising
Using testimonials
Repetition - repetition - repetition
Using pop-ups
Classified ads
Website awards
Ad swaps
Writing an e-book
Backend marketing

Delivering an autoresponder minicourse

Marcia Yudkin is a marketing consultant (**www.yudkin.com/marketing.htm**) author and speaker based in Boston, US. The following copy in the upper-left-hand corner of the navigation bar on her home page caught my eye:

In a rush? Click here to receive a FREE 7-day 'virtual seminar' by e-mail. Learn how to overcome common marketing challenges and redo brochures and sales letters for greater response.

Click and a blank message pops up on your screen, prepopulated with **marketingseminar@getresponse.com** in the To: field. Just hit the Send button, and you'll receive daily, for one week, Marcia's seven-part 'Marketing Makeover' course. Each daily lesson is written in a digestible length of about 700 words, and includes an example of a collateral sales piece that she critiques and improves. A couple of best practices: The subject headings are all the same except for the number of the lesson. Each message is organised and formatted identically, so you know where to find what e.g., introductory information and she includes a phone number as well as a personal email address if you want more information.

Multilevel membership programs

Advertising is no longer enough to support information-based websites. Membership and subscription plans can help you continue to make money. Consider adding a multilevel membership program to boost your profits more. Here's how it works. In this example, you have a password-protected area of your website, a newsletter, and three e-books. The first level of membership would receive your newsletter. The second ('silver', 'deluxe' or 'advanced') level of membership would include your newsletter plus your password-protected website. The third ('gold', 'premium' or 'diamond') level of membership would include your newsletter, password-protected website plus all your e-books.

You can create your memberships to comprise any combination of products and/or services. You just need the next level of membership to have something more valuable (an upsell). You convince your prospective customers that they need the basic version, and then try to sell them a more expensive one with more benefits. Here are some things you can sell to members:

Your time, e.g. half hour of consulting	Password-protected articles
Discussion list	Special reports or electronic books
Templates or step-by-step instructions	Members-only bulletin board
Telephone, chat, videoconferencing	Webinars
Video or audiotapes	Resource list
Newsletter	Tips lists
Frequently Asked Questions list	Freebies
Answers to email or telephone questions	

Here are some of the benefits to you:

- You make money. If your information is unique and valuable, you can charge £50 or more for a basic membership, and you get to charge them again every year. You can make money sending your members special offers from other companies or promoting more of your own products or services.
- Members are more loyal than customers – they have made an investment in your company. They will buy from you again and again.
- You build a list of people interested in your products and services.

Diversify!

Do you have a fantastic product? Create a line of products to augment it and sign up for affiliate programs, which complement it. If your website is designed to attract leads, add more methods and reasons for people to send you their information. Consider adding a newsletter, feedback form, free report, or email course. Make visitors give you their names and email addresses to download the free program, ebook or screensaver you offer.

Using seminars to generate leads

Currently there's a duel between seminars on terra firma and online webinars. At the time of writing, market leaders such as MarketFirst (**www.marketfirst.com**) is offering an on-the-ground seminar and Responsys.com (**www.responsys.com**) a webinar. So which type of venue is more effective in generating leads?

MarketFirst recently ran an email campaign that resulted in an unexpectedly high number of conversions. The hope was that 1,200 people would sign up for a free, offline seminar over a period of three months. Instead, according to Director of Marketing, Scott Leatherman, registration was at 1,900 after only one month. Why such high conversion numbers? Possibly the quality of the messages MarketFirst sent in addition to the richness of the offer.

MarketFirst used the technique of writing their acquisition message as if it were a retention communication to an existing customer. If you follow this idea, include useful, highly relevant content and avoid being sales-y. Your communication has to appear seamless, from the click that opens your email message to the registration on the landing page. The MarketFirst message started off with 'Dear (your first name),' followed by a recent factoid from a Jupiter Research (**www.jup.com**) report asserting the cost effectiveness and high response rate of email marketing (offers credibility of MarketFirst's message). Next we learn that marketing automation can be phenomenally effective if it's done correctly. And then come the offers, primary and secondary. The primary offer is a personal invitation ('you are invited') to a seminar near you, run by industry experts and 'sponsored by MarketFirst Software.' There's even a one-sentence bio of the expert leading your seminar, along with links to the bios of other speakers. Another link directs you to the news and events page of MarketFirst's site, giving you the times and geographic locations of upcoming seminars as well as information on related tradeshows and conferences sponsored by other organisations.

Now comes the secondary offer: If you show up in the flesh at the seminar you register for, you will receive a free copy of B2B marketing guru Barry Silverstein's book, 'Business to Business Internet Marketing: Seven Proven Strategies for Increasing Profits Through Internet Direct Marketing.' The invitation letter is signed by Scott Leatherman and includes a direct phone number for those who prefer to register by phone.

Finally less than 24 hours later, MarketFirst sent an automated thank-you with your registration information. Included again was the link to the seminar information and location page.

The webinar is seen as the latest and greatest way to generate qualified leads. Responsys.com is currently running an email campaign, using a PostMaster Direct.com opt-in list. Like MarketFirst's, the email message is straightforward and credible and includes a double offer. In this case, it's a free, downloadable white paper (in PDF format) along with an invitation to 'join' Responsys.com's CEO in an 'online seminar' on a particular date. When you click to the landing page, you realise that the company is also pushing sign-ups to this page through a direct-mail campaign. Does it mean we're on the 'B' list if we didn't get the mailed invitation? The copy tries to make us feel OK about this: 'If you did not receive a mailed letter invite, you can also register by simply entering the word 'guest.'"

Get creative with ad units and placement

We all know how annoying pop-up boxes or orange blobs dancing across our screens can be. On the flip side, a strategically placed Flash application or superstitial can be extremely effective especially when it comes to branding or imprinting a URL. Site integration anywhere, except in that top-of-the-page banner slot, makes perfect sense. Text links can work beautifully. Or imagine what a banner that appeared in the middle of a search results page on a search engine might look like, say after the third or fourth search result. You're still in that above the fold space, but you're integrated. Below the fold can work, too. Confirmation pages, whether for checking your free email account or entering a sweepstakes, are great locations. Someone has just completed an action. What are they going to do next? Click on your ad unit. It's all about contextual integration coupled with a strong call to action.

Freebie marketing ploys

Make sure that your free service is closely related to what you are selling so the visitors you attract will be good prospects for your business. Give visitors multiple opportunities and links to cross over to the sales part of your site. Some ideas for freebies include:

- A free report will help you rake in names and addresses, qualify the names and addresses as belonging to people interested in your products and services, and even sell your product or service. Ideally, your free report will offer information of immediate use to your prospective clients. This assures that the names you have collected by offering your free report are potential clients and not just any one off the street. If your free report is an e-book, especially if it is an executable file, it qualifies as a 'free program.' Contact freebie directories and ask them to list your free report. Your report must contain information valuable to your prospective clients, but it must also contain a pitch for your products and services. It must explain why your readers cannot afford to pass up the opportunity you are giving them. Repeat your offer. Remind them of the deadline. Send them at least two follow-up letters or email messages. Offering a free report can be completely automated. Using a follow up autoresponder, you can have your free report and follow up messages sent whenever someone fills out the form on your website or sends an email to your autoresponder.

- Find a great freebie your customers can use already on the internet and make a deal with the owner to offer it on your website (customised, if possible). This could be something related to your product or service like an e-book on the same topic as your website.

- Make your own freebie. You can make your own e-book, clip art or screensaver.

- If you would like your gift to be more physical, you can give your visitors a craft they can print and assemble, such as bookmarks, gift bags or boxes.

- Buy something to give your customers. You can buy the licence to an e-book or software program and offer it for free to your visitors.

- You could even buy something small imprinted with your logo and mail it to your customers. Popular items include mugs, T-shirts, and mouse pads.

Running a contest

People like getting something free. If you publicise a contest available on your site, you'll generate more traffic than normal. Starting a new contest is a great reason to send out press releases to your local offline and online media, which focus on your industry.

Tailor your message and goals for different types of sites

On many sites, you may not be able to get someone to click away, but perhaps you can get visitors to take 30 seconds from their visit to interact with a strategically placed banner or larger ad unit. Entice them to enter a sweepstakes, take a survey, or play a game - all on the host site. Capture their email, and you can follow up with a targeted email message. Your goal should be to get someone to pause for a moment, interact briefly with your brand, and give you just enough information for future follow-up. Remember, too, that in addition to building brand awareness, your ad unit should also imprint your URL on people's minds. Visitors may not be predisposed to visit at that very minute, but they may happily visit at their leisure if they can remember the URL.

Four ways to publicise your content:

1. Jazz up your current advertising. Do you have ads in ezines, magazines, or newspapers? Give readers an offer they can't refuse by telling them about your contest!
2. Take advantage of your current visitors. Are you collecting your visitors' contact information? A contest will encourage more people to give you their mailing addresses, phone numbers, and email addresses.
3. Take advantage of strategic partnership opportunities. Multiply your leads by offering your product or service as a prize to another company with a similar target audience in exchange for the names of participants, or get another company to sponsor your contest (give you a prize to offer participants for free) in exchange for the list of participants.
4. You might consider having a new contest periodically to use these promotion methods over and over. Each contest will lose its heat after a while, and starting a new one with a new prize will interest new potential visitors, customers, and clients.

There are thousands of directories on the internet dedicated to helping people find contests. If your product or service is geared toward a broad audience (especially an audience of bargain hunters or contest junkies), these websites offer an excellent promotional opportunity for your website. Besides referring you leads, their links to you will improve your positions in search engines.

Writing articles

Do you write articles and offer them for free on your website? Not only are articles great for increasing your traffic from search engines and encouraging visitors to return for new information, they're also good excuses to plaster your URL all over the internet! Many websites will want to link to your articles or offer them on their websites. Just make sure your contact information is posted with it, including a link to your website, to boost your website's popularity! List your articles as reasons for related websites to link to you. Add your article to article libraries and directories where publishers often visit to find new content for their newsletters and ezines. List your articles in ezines and on websites offering free articles to ezine publishers and webmasters. Most sites that allow authors to submit articles review the submissions, edit the articles and then schedule them for publication. Once you've established a relationship with a site's editor, and have shown you can continually submit well-written articles, your chances of being published increase considerably. Here are some tips:

- Ask about style and submission guidelines. Some of the basic style issues that will come up in most articles submitted to internet publications include capitalisation and hyphenation (Internet or internet, online or on-line, email or e-mail, etc.).
- Follow basic grammar rules.
- Keep your writing brief. The whole idea of the internet is to disseminate information quickly. There's little point in having readers find an article that is several pages long or requires the reader to scroll down forever. Some publications like to use bulleted or numbered lists, which make information easy to digest. Keep your paragraphs short.
- Stay away from gimmicks that belong in advertising copy. Forget the ALL CAPITAL LETTERS and exclamation points!!! You're not trying to hawk something in a radio ad, you're writing an intelligent article that will benefit your readers, so why are you yelling at them?
- Don't be a nag over most changes. It's okay to ask editors to run major changes by you for approval, but editors are usually professionals.
- Be an editor yourself. Use your spellchecker, and have someone else read your article before you send it. (Remember that spellcheckers will tell you whether a word is spelled correctly, but not whether it is the right word in that context!) If there's no one available, put the article aside and return to it the next day with a fresh set of eyes.
- Make the article as professional as possible. Keep in mind that you're likely to be competing with other authors and articles for space on an online publication. As a general rule, the better the site or newsletter, the more contributions it will have. And that means only the best will be chosen. Do not write a long ad for your business. The best articles are largely unbiased and discuss an area with which the author is familiar, not just their product or service.

Getting your name (and URL) in print publications by writing articles, or getting interviewed offline allows you to reach new, potentially larger audiences than online advertising. The cheapest and easiest way to get your name out is to attract interviews. If you can think of a timely, newsworthy topic involving your expertise, send press releases to newspapers, TV, radio and/or magazines that publish similar stories. You can fax them from your computer or hire a professional to do it for you. Another way to get interviews is to achieve and maintain top search engine rankings for your field. When your subject comes up, reporters will find you. Each interview can lead to more interviews from reporters seeing your name in print as an expert in the field.

If you're interested in reading more about improving your writing, here are some links that may interest you: **The Poynter Report, Summer 2001: Seven Habits for Highly Effective Writing: www.poynter.org/special/ poynterreport; 10 Tips for Writing Powerful Articles: www.selfgrowth. com/articles/Pollock9.html**

Levi's promoting jeans with site film

Levi's is promoting its SILVERTAB line of jeans with a new online campaign that combines a variety of regularly updated interactive elements. At the LostChange campaign site, users are posed the question: 'What would you do if you found $100,000?' The brand's episodic LostChange campaign answers that query through a combination of plot-driven ads and an internet film. The 'LostChange' film, about a group of friends who find a great sum of money and is being released as a series of short weekly episodes, with supporting mission debriefs and rewards. Viewers of the series are intended to become active participants, working to find clues and tracking the friends' whereabouts. The multi-level interactive experience includes games and prizes, including CDs; Motorola two-way pagers, V.100 cell phones and T900 TALKABOUT radios; and SILVERTAB clothing. The site also includes online shopping, featuring the showcased Motorola gadgets and SILVERTAB clothing.

Banners

Of the many banner exchange programs, LinkExchange is the biggest (**www.linkexchange.com**). Essentially, you agree to show a rotating banner on your site for other LinkExchange members, and they do the same for you, and there's a possibility you'll earn something through paid banner ads, too.

A full list of banner exchange programs can be found at **http://bannertips.com/exchangenetworks.shtml**.

Banners account for less than half of all online advertising, but more than half of all B2B online ads are direct response. The Interactive Advertising Bureau reported in April 2001 that online advertising in 2000 reached $8.2 billion, up from $4.6 billion the prior year. Although this was a 78 percent increase, the IAB said that it was lower than in past years. Banner advertising made up 47 percent of the year's ad revenue, with sponsorships accounting for 28 percent. AdRelevance says that about 54 percent of B2B online ads are direct response ads, mostly to drive traffic to web sites. IT companies, most of them being B2B marketers, are more successful than others in using online advertising, according to a May 2001 study by Nielsen/NetRatings. Nevertheless, the study suggests that banner ads are run too frequently on sites with limited audiences, concluding that this causes click-through rates to plummet. Nielsen//NetRatings also says that online advertising frequency rates are in the high teens versus three to four percent in offline advertising.

You may need to spend money to boost traffic by purchasing banner advertising. Choose sites that seem to attract the kinds of people who would be good prospects for your business or product. You can find media brokers who can help you find appropriate and cost-effective places to advertise. Banner ads are the most popular way to promote a website on the internet. If you don't mind putting random banners on your home page, shop around for the free banner exchange program with the best exchange rate or the option of targeting your banners – only running your banners on websites with content relevance to your website. If you want to eventually charge for banner space on your website, don't use free exchanges. Look for websites with content related to your own, decent traffic, and low banner advertisement rates. Offer to exchange banners with them for a short period of time.

Banner ads are not just static 460 x 80 pixel boxes any more. They can range from sophisticated rich-media animations to simple product links. Ford bought a single day's ownership of the Yahoo! home page. It then ran a horizontal banner featuring perched birds that, at first glance, looked quite plain. But before the consumer could enter a search term, the birds flew across the screen and pecked at a pile of birdseed in the lower right corner until they had uncovered a picture of a Ford Explorer. If the consumer clicked on the picture, the screen shook and emitted the noise of a revving engine when suddenly a Ford explorer broke through the page. Ford's unconventional banner ad garnered a 1.28 percent click rate, which is impressive considering the tens of millions of daily visitors to Yahoo!. In total, almost 250,000 consumers were driven to the Ford Outfitters web site via the 'bird-board' ad that day.

Fake campaign yields real banner ad info

Banners do brand, according to new research from Dynamic Logic and interactive agency eBrands. The research is based on the results from an advertising campaign for a fictitious new brand: YesSirNoSir, a personal concierge service. The companies found awareness levels for the brand were raised from 4 percent (baseline) to 11 percent overall (among those exposed to the online ads). Awareness levels were even higher (just over 19 percent) among the target demographic group (professionals age 18-49). As seen in other studies, there was a positive correlation between the frequency of exposure and branding levels.

The brand was advertised exclusively online across the UK properties of iVillage.com and FTMarketWatch.com. The campaign of 2 million impressions ran over May and early June 2001 - an estimated $70,000 worth of media. Dynamic Logic used the campaign to test the value of online advertising's ability to build brand without the support of traditional advertising.

Only buy banner space from websites with content which attracts the sort of visitors you want on your website – the kind which will be interested in your products or services. Try to find the best banner advertisement rates from those websites. The best deals are often where the site charges only for the people who click on your banner. Banner advertising is best for branding. However banner links on web sites are less effective than text links. More people will click on a text link than a banner. With text links, you are able to pre-qualify people before they visit your affiliate partner's site, and you will find that more convert to sales.

Click-throughs are a misleading indicator of banner effectiveness. A June 2001 study of banner branding in Europe, the first of its kind, was conducted by XXIST.Com (now defunct), Engage, and just-sites.com, a business knowledge provider with multiple sites. Banner ads were created displaying the site logo, the URL of the target site, and a strong branding statement, but no call to action. Sites that ran the banners did not have any hyperlinks to the destination sites. No additional offline or online advertising or promotion was executed during the campaign or in the month preceding the campaign. The results of this study indicated that nearly half of the responses to the campaign came from people who saw the banner but did not click on it. And 60 percent of these indirect responders arrived at the destination site within 24 hours of seeing the ad. Indirect responders were more likely to return to the destination site than those who clicked on the banner.

As the study's conclusion pointed out, had the campaign been analysed purely on click-through rate, or even post-click conversion rate, the campaign would have 'failed.' By aggregating and tracking the direct and indirect response data, this campaign achieved half the cost per acquisition compared with that of direct response only.

Affiliate programmes

Essentially, a retailer's affiliate program pays a commission to other sites whose links to the retailer result in an actual sale. The goal is to build a network of affiliates who have a financial stake in promoting your site. If you're a merchant you need to:

1   determine the commission you are willing to pay (consider it your advertising cost)
2   select a company to set up the technical details of your program
3   promote your program to get the right kind of affiliates who will link to your site.

Two affiliate programs to consider:

1. Commission Junction (**www.cj.com/go.asp?69320**) sets up the entire program for the merchant, handles administrative details, and pays the affiliates
2. AffiliateZone (**www.affiliatezone.com/al/affiliates.cgi?225**) installs excellent software on your site to allow you to track purchases through affiliate links, and enable you to administer the program yourself

Here's how affiliate programs work. The website designer creates or installs a program on their host server which allows visitors to fill out a form and become affiliates or associates of the website. The program posts their vital information on the server and tracks the traffic (or purchases) each affiliate brings to the website. The websites offering affiliate programs pay their affiliates for the traffic they bring, sometimes limiting the payment by only offering it for paying customers or even first-time customers.

Successful affiliate programs are more effective than banner advertising on popular, targeted websites or top listings in search engines for bringing in orders because they encourage other webmasters to use their promotion skills and visitor loyalty to bring new, targeted visitors to the website offering them. Affiliate programs made Amazon.com successful. It's like having a voluntary sales force working solely on commission! There are a lot of ways to set up an affiliate program. You must decide whether or not to screen applicants, what you are going to pay them for, and how much you will pay. You must also decide how much you will help your affiliates 'sell' your website. Are you going to give them a banner? A button? Will you offer internet marketing tips or link to pages that do?

Some websites (and affiliates) see affiliates as sales representatives who work on commissions. The websites who offer affiliate programs don't need to pay salaries, so it doesn't matter whether the affiliates are good marketers, as long as there are a lot of them. On the other hand, if you don't screen your affiliates, you may end up with some unethical people spamming in the name of your company. Be sure to make your marketing guidelines clear. Don't send unsolicited email, and don't allow anyone else to do it on your company's behalf. Potential visitors are already becoming wary of websites set up just to take advantage of affiliate programs. Affiliates must offer more, like links to the best-priced items.

If you offer a service or products with appeal to a limited audience, you might benefit more from a good reciprocal link program (and they're cheaper), but if you do start an affiliate program, screen your applicants carefully and only allow a few websites to join. The better you can monitor your affiliates and the way they are promoting your website, the more your program will pay off. Additionally, affiliate programs are difficult to set up, so small businesses may find affiliate programs too expensive.

If you want to join some affiliate programs, don't just affiliate with websites that offer you the most money. Look for quality websites which will improve your visitors' experience at your website. Make sure the affiliate programs you wish to join are reputable and offer reasonable amounts of money. Most of all, don't destroy your visitors' experience with flashy affiliate-program banners which increase the load time of your website. If you want money, and don't mind the banners, sell advertising space. Give text links for affiliate programs, working them into the content of your website naturally.

AOL marketing new Madonna tour

America Online is becoming an extremely popular promotional partner for pop music performers launching a new album or tour. Recent recipients of marketing support from AOL have included singer Janet Jackson and rapper P. Diddy. Now, you can add Madonna to the list. AOL is offering members a 'Madonna All-Access' to help promote the pop-star's first US tour in eight years. Through AOL Keyword: Madonna, members will find concert footage from Barcelona, exclusive, unreleased photos of Madonna including live performance pictures from Europe, Madonna music videos and an updated version of 'Madonna's Mix' on Spinner.com that features a collection of Madonna's songs and the music that influenced her. Also, weekly sweepstakes winners will fly to see Madonna perform in concert. AOL's promotion of Madonna's tour is part of the company's tour sponsorship. The mega-ISP will be involved in on-site promotions at concert venues and will also be prominently displayed in the Madonna tour book.

More visitors will click on text links (especially if you offer testimonials). Unless your website is your business, and advertising is the way you make money, the less advertising and affiliates you have, the better. Always do what's best for the design and content of your website. Adding an affiliate program to your site is like asking 1000 people to walk into your office tomorrow and asking if they can work for you for nothing. You pay by performance only.

Paid advertising

Some form of paid advertising is important if you wish to grow your business, since paid advertising motivates others to carry your marketing message to their own networks of site visitors and e-mail newsletter recipients. Here are three types of advertising for the small businesses:

Cost per action advertising

Cost per action/acquisition (CPA) advertising is often known as affiliate program advertising. While the set-up fees to begin your own program may vary, such a program allows you to recruit and pay affiliates only when a link on their site results in a sale or sign-up on your website. Your goal is to find an effective form of advertising for your goods and services that is affordable from a cost-per-sale perspective and therefore sustainable on a month-to-month basis.

Sponsorships and CPM advertising

Traditional advertising pays the publisher to carry an ad in the publication priced in proportion to how many people are likely to see the ad – readers, subscribers, etc. It is often sold on a CPM (cost per thousand impressions) basis. Another approach to paid advertising is to purchase an ad for a fixed cost per week or per issue, no matter how many visitors or subscribers happen to see it. Look for newsletters related to your site and investigate ad prices for small ads.

Cost per click advertising

One very popular small business approach is to pay for advertising on a cost per click basis (CPC). The best known of CPC sites is GoTo.com (**www.goto.com**) where you can bid on search terms. There are many similar sites (**www.payperclicksearchengines.com**) that have no minimum bid, though none with the reach of GoTo.com. However, since you only pay when someone clicks through, you can save money by using a combination of these less-visited sites with lower bid prices for keywords.

Look for media deals. Make sure online advertising works harder by building in a direct-response component. Consider email newsletter ads and search engine ads as potential online advertising alternatives. New ad sizes are more effective. Despite the higher cost of new, larger online ads, such as skyscrapers, these advertising vehicles seem to be resulting in higher click-throughs. A July 2001 study by CNet suggests that the new ad units enhance aided and unaided brand recall by as much as 55 percent and positively impact consideration of brand purchase after one exposure. In July 2001, the IAB cited three studies that attest to the success of new, larger online ads. One survey of 8,750 web users shows that larger ads are 25 percent more effective than banner ads at raising brand awareness and message association. Most effective are skyscraper ads. Another study, commissioned by Doubleclick, reports an 86 percent boost in brand awareness from larger ads versus 56 percent with banner ads. Move to bigger ad units, or at least test them against banners. Consider the impact of ad size on awareness. Look for opportunities to pinpoint your media buy, taking ad space on well-targeted sites that address audiences important to your marketing efforts.

Using testimonials

An extremely powerful marketing tool to use is the testimonial. According to marketing guru Dan Kennedy, 'What others say about you and your product, service, or business is at least 1000% more convincing than what you say, even if you are 1000% more eloquent.' The reason is obvious. Customers doubt what we say about ourselves, but believe other customers. And the more customers who say good things about us, the more prospective customers will believe them.

Time management consultant Larry Dolan told marketing guru Dan Kennedy he closes every inquiry he gets for a speaking engagement. He has no brochure, no demo tape, and no videotape. When a prospective client calls, Larry simply sends a hand-addressed box of copies of testimonial letters. Can you imagine the power of hundreds of letters praising his presentation? This is more compelling and believable than anything Larry could say about himself.

How can you get testimonials? First, you must provide an outstanding product and service. Interview your customers about what they really like about your product and the service you provide. What do they especially like about working with you and your company? Ask if they would write what they told you in a letter or if you can write it for them for their approval.

Repetition – repetition – repetition

A business mails a sales letter to a list. It has a response that more than pays for the advertising expense, but stops after only making one mailing. By continuing the campaign by repeating the offer again and again, it could multiply its response. For example, it might get 1% response on the first mailing, 1 % on the second, and 2 % on the third. If it stopped after the first mailing, it would have reduced its results by 75 percent! People's situations are constantly changing. Maybe they didn't want your product or service before, but now they're in the market.

For example, if you were in the computer sales business, your prospect might have had an interest in new computers before, but had no urgency to act. After your first contact, his computer broke down for the umpteenth time. Now he is in the market and ready to buy! You need to be in your customers' faces regularly so you will be there when they are ready to take action.

Second, your customer might not have seen the letter or ad! Her spouse might have thrown it away. She might have been busy and 'screened it out.' When you continue sending the material, you dramatically increase the likelihood your prospective customer will actually see it! As long as the economics work. If you get no response from your first effort, and it was sizable enough to be a legitimate test, throw it out! If you get a response that justifies the expense, continue it as long as it pays for itself.

Many charities have found that they have a loss from the first donation from a donor. They make their money from continuing to get donations from people who donated before.

Using pop-ups

Have you ever loaded a home page, and a pop-up ad appears in the upper left-hand corner of the browser, and then moves behind the browser as another pop-up identical to the first appears in front of the browser again? I did this and clicked shut the top ad, not aware of the one hiding behind the browser, which I discovered only when I finally closed the browser. Annoying or what! In another visit to a home page, a large pop-up ad window appeared over the left side of my browser. When I moved my cursor over there to close it, it disappeared and reappeared over the centre of my browser. This kind of pop-up behaviour suggests a degree of contempt for the customer. It also shows an inability to choose between the good and bad opportunities offered by the internet. So if you want some pop-ups on your site, what do you do?

Because they are inexpensive and easy to install and uninstall, pop-up windows, also called interstitials, are an attractive advertising tool for small businesses. But like all advertising techniques, pop-ups must be used appropriately to be effective. In general, successful pop-ups have the following characteristics:

- Use your pop-up to encourage visitors to perform a specific action. Visitors tend to ignore advertisements, but they respond positively to pop-ups that offer the opportunity to participate in a survey or subscribe to a newsletter.
- They offer tangible benefits. According to Isabel Gonzales, director of corporate marketing at Internet marketing firm AdFlight, some of the most effective pop-up ads are used to provide information, such as about a company. Successful pop-ups give the customer an incentive, such as a gift, a coupon or a report.
- They are highly targeted and should be aimed at a specific audience and have a specific purpose. A pop-up successfully appeals to a target demographic e.g. people interested in receiving information about a specific topic. You can use cookies to personalise pop-ups for individual users.

Unsuccessful pop-ups often have one or more of the following characteristics:

- They offer irrelevant information such as advertisements for unrelated products, which distract visitors.

- Customers seem to find so-called 'hard sell' pop-ups particularly irritating.

- Pop-up ads have a bad reputation because they distract the viewer, interrupting whatever was going on at the time, such as purchasing.

- An added drawback to pop-up windows is that they can have a negative impact on search engine and directory listings.

- Even if no rules forbid pop-ups, directory editors frown on them.

Whether pop-ups work magic for your business depends on how you use them and on your audience. Some people are more irritated by pop-ups than others. How do you know whom pop-up ads will annoy? You can find out by testing them on a limited audience. Set the JavaScript so the ads appear to 10 percent of your audience, for example. Then wait to see what kind of feedback you get.

Classified ads

Free classified ads websites are a lot like Free For All Links pages – they are created to boost traffic of their host website by offering free promotion of other peoples' websites. Classified ads do not always offer a link to your website, and you must submit an advertisement rather than a website description. If you have a product or service, which should appeal to a mass audience and experience writing successful, short ads, free classified ads may work for you. Remember to find places to advertise where your target audience hangs out. Most of the people visiting classified ad websites are those coming to submit their website's classified ad.

Mobile ads help Jeep launch new vehicle

DaimlerChrysler is promoting its newest Jeep vehicle with a two-month wireless advertising effort. Mobile infrastructure company AvantGo is hosting the campaign for the Jeep Liberty on its mobile internet service. As part of the campaign, the Jeep brand will be collecting information and an e-mail address from potential new customers in the form of a mobile device questionnaire. 'Wireless is an increasingly important part of any digital marketing strategy. This is especially true in the case of our all-new Jeep Liberty,' says Diane Jackson, of Jeep Brand marketing communications. 'AvantGo has helped make wireless advertising an attractive and easy way to build brand awareness and reach the younger, more technologically savvy Jeep Liberty buyer. This is the first wireless advertising campaign for the Jeep brand, and we believe that it strongly supports our traditional advertising initiatives by placing our message in front of our target in a new way.'

Website awards

Many websites offer awards to the best websites and list links to past winners. Winners get an implied testimonial, if not a real one. Winning an award can be even better than getting a link from another website, since they give you an icon to display on your site to show that Important People like your web design.

If you happen to find an award site, apply. Otherwise, save time by applying for awards with the Awards Worksheet **websiteawards.xe.net** – whenever you make big changes to your website. Only apply for the most highly ranked awards, and awards that apply specifically to your industry. Web site awards can be found in all shapes and sizes. There are the awards that all serious web page writers want to win which are normally awarded by recognisable and reputable bodies, possibly profession-based or technology-based. Then you get the awards that are primarily set up by people wanting to attract visitors to their own site by including a hyperlink in the awards graphic. Almost anyone applying for an award given out by webmasters (who have little or no interest in the award other than as a means to attract visitors to their own site) will win!

Some award sites worth visiting include:

FT International Business Website of the Year
www.businesswebawards.com/

Worldbest Websites
www.worldbestwebsites.com/

The ISI/InterForum E-Commerce Awards
www.isi-interforum-awards.com

TPM Online
www.philosophers.co.uk/awards/htm
> (offers gold, silver and bronze awards)

Website Awards Worksheet
www.dlb99.com/web_award/hosts/hvworksheet.html
> (you can download a worksheet and apply to over 800 award sites around the world)

Ad swaps

Ezine advertisements are some of the most effective paid advertising opportunities on the internet, and you can get them free. All you need is your own ezine to take advantage of this opportunity for free traffic. For best results, your ezine should contain valuable information for subscribers and feature regular advertisements. That means you must have advertisements in your ezine in the same spot every week, and preferably the same number of them, whether you're paid for them or not.

While your ezine is small (less than 100 subscribers), fill the space with advertisements for affiliate programs you've signed up for that relate to your ezine's topic. Once you have some subscribers (not necessarily 100), start asking related publications for ad swaps. You can find related publications in ezine directories, ad swap ezines, ezine announcement lists, and on websites you discover in the normal course of business. Ad swap ezines can be particularly effective, since you see immediately the number of subscribers to each ezine, its topic, and other vital information. The publishers are also already inclined to swap ads and are more likely to be willing to swap ads with smaller publications. Swap Resources (**www.swapresources.com**) and Ezine Swap (**http://ezine-swap.com**) are worth visiting.

Always choose publications reaching your target audience. Related topics work best, but sometimes swapping with an unrelated publication can work even better if they reach the people who would be interested in your topic. Request swaps with publications with a similar number of subscribers, preferably slightly larger publications. If a publication with a smaller subscriber base requests a swap from you, it may still be worth swapping if you've got the space.

If a publication has a much larger subscriber base (say twice as many subscribers), especially if you still have few subscribers, offer to even things out by publishing extra ads for them (maybe 2 for 1) or giving them better exposure with an 'exclusive' ad or the top ad. When sending an email to an editor or publisher to request an ad swap, include the following information:

- where you found their ezine, and praise for it if you've read it
- the name, topic, and frequency of your publication
- your number of subscribers
- a place where the editor or publisher can find or request sample issues
- a short description of your ezine
- your ad, which should preferably match the specifications of the publication you're addressing, but if you don't know the length of the ads they publish, send them one of the lengths you publish.

Don't forget to mention you would like to swap ads, the number of ads you would like to swap, and anything else they should know about your ezine before swapping ads with you. One ad swap is never enough. 3 is a good number, and 5 is better if you have plenty of ad space to swap. If the ads are successful, you may want to swap more or even establish a permanent joint venture.

Writing an e-book

Writing an ebook is not like writing a novel. It can be any length, and you can charge any price (limited only by the value it offers to your buyers). Here is an explanation of how to create an ebook:

1. Get content. It must be content unavailable through traditional print media, and it should be substantially original. If you have written articles (which are no longer published anywhere), given taped lectures, or have catalogs or brochures, compile that material into a book. Or you could get other people to write the content for you. If you have to write new content yourself, get a copy of the special report, 'How to Write A Book On Anything in 14 Days or Less... Guaranteed!? A Guide for Professionals' at **www.writeabooknow.com/welcome/write106now**.

2. Decide on the format of your e-book. There is a variety of e-book software available on the internet. If you have purchased an ebook that had a particularly nice format, ask the author how they did it. If you want to go cheap and easy, you can write your e-book in HTML. It has no copy protection, but it's the universal language of the internet and anyone will be able to read your book without a plug-in or special program. Since you already have a website, you either already know HTML or you have a program that can handle it for you. If you want to offer something classy, use PDF. Adobe Acrobat Reader's format allows you to do everything you can with HTML and you get some copy protection. Nobody can enter your document and change it (unless they own the expensive Adobe Acrobat program). Many programs can export documents as PDF files, including Adobe Pagemaker and Adobe Illustrator.

3. Translate your content into your preferred format, e.g. you could write your book in Word and then import it into Adobe Pagemaker, adding links and a Table of Contents in Pagemaker, then exporting it into PDF. You will likely have to do something similar, either copy-pasting or importing your content into your e-book software then tweaking your text and adding links so it looks right before you save it.

4. Test your ebook. Check the links to be sure they work, and the formatting to make sure your text looks nice and is easy to follow.

5. Load the ebook into a special directory of your website. You can then either allow visitors to download it as a 'freebie' for subscribing to your ezine, sending you contact information, or just visiting your website or you can set up a sales letter and ask your visitors to buy it.

Backend marketing

Are you making the most of your current customers? If your Thank You page and email message don't suggest additional products or services, you're not. If you don't have an email list of current customers whom you email with special offers, you don't. Some hints:

● If you have more than one product, sell the one your new customer hasn't bought on your Thank You page and/or your Thank You email. Keep a list of all the people who have ordered on your website, and send them follow-up email with special offers for your other products or services.

● If you only have one product, how can you use your customer base to make more money? Sell more of the product or service to your customers. When your product is about to run out, make them a special offer to buy more.

- Supposing your product lasts forever, e.g. marble counters. Use your Thank You material and customer list to sell products or services for other companies. Join affiliate programs, or trade advertising space with a related website.

- Have you already joined affiliate programs? Your 'Thank You' material is a great place to promote them. Just make sure the product you're promoting is a good one, and related to the product you've sold.

- Once your customers have received your product, contact them. Leave a note in the box, email them, or even give them a phone call. Ask them if they're satisfied with your product, have any questions, or have any suggestions. Then try to sell them something else. Continue to send your customers special offers and reminders.

- If you can, keep track of which customers have bought what and when. Make sure they get announcements only for related products or services they don't have, or have run out of. Make each message personalised.

LAST MINUTE HINTS AND TIPS

- co-ordinate offline and online brands

- automate your sales force

- recruit affiliate partners to sell your products or services and offer them commission for referrals

- encourage partners to add their own value by putting a certain subset of your products and services in a unique informational context for their specific audience

- offer special deals to most successful partners

- integrate everything your company does online with everything it does offline

- set up feedback loops between different business channels

- maintain customer data for market research

8

Marketing Through Synchronous and Asynchronous Discussion and Newsgroups

CLICK-ONS

Synchronous discussion

Moderating asynchronous discussion

Newsgroups

Synchronous discussion

Web chats are easy for marketers to run and are likely to generate sales leads for you. B2B web chats operate just like B2C web chats that you may have seen at AOL or Yahoo. Visitors log into a chat room online, and post their questions to a moderator. Then the visiting expert types in the answers to the questions.

Chat is a form of synchronous communication (meaning simultaneous) as opposed to asynchronous (at different times) and requires careful planning to ensure that all aspects of the design, scheduling, delivery and management of an event produce successful results.

The advantage to synchronous discussion or chat rooms is instant communication and the opportunity of meeting new people interested in the same subject. The disadvantage is you need a lot of traffic to support continuous activity on your website. If you want a chat room, you will need a popular topic people will want to talk about in person, and you will need to promote it ruthlessly. This method can also be used in combination with asynchronous methods.

Here are some hints about running synchronous discussion easily and effectively:

Designing the session
Decide on the purpose of the session. Is it for: information transmission, discussion, decision-making, voting or education on a specific skill or application? Ask yourself how does it fit into an overall programme of marketing? Determine how many people will be involved. A session to make people aware of a subject can be broadcast to a large audience; a discussion for example, should be limited to fewer than 10 people. Which specific tools will you need to use? Are you going to give a presentation involving PowerPoint slides, make use of an application, or any of the special tools provided with your synchronous product? If you are not an experienced session leader, estimate the time then halve your content.

Scheduling the session
Book the session well in advance and remind people at regular intervals as the date nears. Synchronous sessions should be treated the same as critical meetings which cannot be missed. If it is the first time for many participants, book the session to start half an hour before the real start time. Use that half-hour to test access and use of the tool by the participants. Schedule a chat to last 30, 45 or 60 minutes and choose a day between Tuesday-Thursday. Managers feel they need their mornings free to be productive, and then at 2pm they are just trickling back from lunch. If they are just 5-10 minutes late for the chat, many people won't bother to attend at all. So, try 2:30pm. Warn your Help Desk or any support staff that there may be additional calls during the beginning of the session.

Getting attendance
Market your chat through the media that works best for you. Email,

telemarketing and direct mail all work for different marketers. Send the offer twice to your best list, to get the highest response. To boost response, offer an incentive such as useful white papers featuring information that can improve the bottom line. Don't just publicise a day and time for the chat. Instead, tell people they need to register to attend. Create an auto-email that immediately sends every registrant an official ticket number so they feel they have something tangible. Two/three days prior to the chat, send a reminder email (or telephone call) to registrants that asks, 'if you can't make it, please forward your ticket to someone in your organisation who can.' Send one last reminder email the morning of the event.

Planning the agenda

Prepare an agenda, which lists items with timings and priorities and aim for a maximum of no more than 90 minutes for each session, and preferably less than that. Make your initial session up to 45 minutes. Put high priority items near the beginning of the agenda and break the session down into separate chunks. By mixing activities, you will retain the interest of the participants. Include a number of activities where the participants have to contribute actively. Make any individual presentation less than 7 minutes long, which is about the maximum that people can concentrate in a passive way. If you have more than one presentation segment, insert a discussion or other session between presentations. Allow sufficient time for introductions, questions, interactive elements and closing remarks. Issue the agenda in advance, as well as clear instructions on any preparation the participants will have to make prior to the session commencing. Provide an etiquette document if needed, to guide participants on behaviour and expectations for their contribution to the session.

Preparing the content

Keep your first session short and simple. Once you and the audience are familiar with the technology and its uses, then you can move to more complex sessions. Make graphics simple and easy to read as screen resolutions may vary amongst the participants. Complex slides take longer to download, and if the critical messages are not in the graphics, don't use them.

Do not display large volumes of text and limit any text to no more than half a page, and ensure it is at least 12-point font, preferably larger. It is important to check the timings of these segments, and allow for the fact that there may be many questions during the live session. If possible, practice complex activities in a realistic as possible situation, with one or two other participants located at different physical sites.

Invite guest speakers to provide variety and interest for the audience. It is advisable for the expert to have a training session prior to the event, or to be located with someone who is familiar with the tools, so that he or she can focus on the content of the session. Send out some preparatory work for the participants. Ask them to come with 3-5 questions on the subject, a number of brainstorm ideas, a summary of an opinion on a document, or a priority list of discussion items. It will help to ensure participation is active and includes most members of the audience.

Running the session

Some tips include:

- Allow participants to choose whether they'd like to be anonymous or not.
- Let everyone know at the start of the chat that they will receive a transcript afterwards. This allows them to relax and participate, rather than worry about taking notes.
- Let everyone know that all pertinent questions will be answered, even if there's not enough time during the chat itself. You can add on answers to extra questions to the end of the transcript afterwards. Some companies even allow attendees up to 10 days after the event to send in follow-up questions.
- Warn your visiting expert that you prefer all acronyms and other shortened technical terms to be spelled out whenever possible.
- Get a list of URLs that your visiting expert might link to, and check them for accuracy prior to the chat.
- Provide a warm welcome and mention participants by name or location. If numbers and time allow let participants introduce themselves.
- Stick to your agenda. If participants are having technical difficulties that cannot be resolved before the session starts, refer them to Help Desk or other support.
- Provide a quick review of the tool and your expectations of the participants before you start.
- Speak clearly and in a normal voice. Make sure you are the correct distance from the microphone. One of the most common problems encountered in these sessions is caused by excessive speed, the facilitator talking too quickly and/or rushing through the material. Do not use acronyms that the participants may not understand, and take care over your use of language, which might offend. Keep instructions clear

and concise and repeat them in a different format if needed.

- Be aware of distractions, which could affect the quality of the transmissions, such as external noise, moving away from the microphone, rustling paper, and tapping the table. If you are using video, then make sure there are no distracting visual images in view.
- If side conversations are allowed, ensure that a 'microphone off/mute' feature is used.
- Poll the audience for feedback frequently. If you have a large audience, you may want to ask for questions by group/location.
- Make sure you mention names of participants, so they feel included. Ask participants to introduce themselves by name before making a comment; if they do not, make sure that you name them when you reply.
- Allow for a 1-second delay in transmission to the audience. If you are combining audio and visual images, make sure that you leave enough time for them to appear synchronised at the receiving end. Introduce items in general terms verbally, announcing your actions, whilst allowing time for the images to appear visually. If possible, arrange to download large files to the learners before the session begins.
- Do not interrupt speakers unless it is necessary. Recognise that due to transmission delays, interruptions may occur at inappropriate times.
- Keep the session on track and keep an eye on the time.
- Close the session formally with an item such as survey or vote on effectiveness.

Reviewing the session

Once the session is over, assess and review it, then share your experiences with other facilitators and document plans for improvement for future sessions. If you have recorded any of your session, you may be able to use the recording to help others learn synchronous session facilitation skills. Use telephone or written surveys to ask the participants for more extensive feedback than you may have received during the actual session. Send every participant a thank you note after the chat. When possible include a personal note about the participant's contributions such as 'Your question on XYZ was a valuable one.' Instead of sending the transcript as-is, bear in mind your company's professionalism will be judged by it. So, have a grammatical expert clean up punctuation, spelling and any incorrect URLs first. Plus, add in explanations for any acronyms or jargon. Then, after including additional questions that came in after the chat, send a copy of the transcript to all attendees in a format that's easy to read such as Word. You should also consider sending a copy of the transcript, or a link to where it sits on your site, to everyone who couldn't make the chat itself. Let them know you're sorry they couldn't make it; you hope they'll find this valuable and you hope to see them next time.

Build community through a bulletin board

A website bulletin board allows visitors to post a message on your website and respond to other people's messages. Once you set one up, you'll have an administrative panel, which will allow you to move and remove posts. They are easy to maintain, and you could even get your visitors to do the work for you, while you sit back and collect the money (from advertising or products sold on other parts of your website) and maintain quite a bit of control.

Moderating asynchronous discussion

Asynchronous discussion happens at different times with messages sometimes not being acknowledged or responded to for days or weeks by conference participants. Some hints include:

Have clear objectives	Participants must believe their online interactions are time well spent.
Preparation time	Planning, developing and distributing materials need a substantial lead-time.
Have experienced facilitators	Avoid having a first-time facilitator working online the first time.
Develop a common reader	A common reader that addresses both the content and any common technical concerns is important. These could serve as the basis for discussion, provide introductory information, description of activities and resources materials.
Distribute a list of participants	Make available to all subscribers to the conference, a list of participants so that private messages can be addressed to individuals and not to the list.
Use introductions	The facilitator should encourage the participants to

introduce themselves, to help build the sense of community.

Encourage participation The use of various learning options can stimulate participation and interaction through small group discussion, debates, polling activities and one-on-one message exchanges.

Maintain a non-authoritarian style It is usually better to avoid the authority figure role when facilitating online.

Make the material relevant Develop questions and activities for participants that relate to their experiences.

Required contributions With some computer conferencing systems, it may be appropriate to require a participant to respond to the topic or question under discussion before he/she can access the answers posted by other participants.

Be objective Before generalising to the conference about a contribution, consider such things as the tone and content of the posting, the author and his/her skills, knowledge and attitudes that you may know about from prior conference postings, and time of the posting in relation to the conference thread.

Don't expect too much Facilitators need to be content if two or three well-articulated, major points are communicated in a particular thread of discussion.

Don't rely on offline materials Summarise the assigned readings online so that the discussion remains mostly self-contained.

Promote private conversations Design opportunities for private conversations among two or more people who you suspect have similar interests in the content.

Find unifying threads Facilitators can weave several strands of conversation into a summarisation that may prompt people to pursue the topic further.

Present conflicting opinions Facilitators can draw attention to opposing perspectives, different directions, or conflicting opinions that could lead to debates and peer critiques.

Watch the use of humour/sarcasm	It may be wise not to use humour or sarcasm due to different cultural and ethnic backgrounds that may be represented. Using text-based communications, it is especially difficult to construe intent and tone from on-screen text, unless you know the participants very well.
Facilitate interactivity	A sense of interactive participation is often promoted by using special introductory techniques, dyadic partnering, and some activities that facilitated informal discussion among participants.
Maintain flexibility	Because of the individuality of the participants, content need to remain flexible and the facilitator need to support this. Rather than presenting an elaborate seminar agenda at the outset, follow the flow of the conversation, while guiding it toward the subject.
Invite visiting experts	Guest experts may join the conference with participants to respond to posted contributions, or so participants can ask questions of the visitor.
Don't lecture	Experience strongly suggests that a long, elaborate, logically coherent sequence of comments yields silence. Instead, use open-ended remarks, examples, and weaving to elicit comment and other views.
Request responses	The facilitator may ask particular participants for comments on a topic or question, then give them time to respond.
Be accepting of lurkers	Recognise that there will be 'lurkers' in the conference and they may never participate with comments. Both lurkers (or any latecomers to the session) must be acknowledged and welcomed.
Model the behaviour you seek	Reinforcing and modelling good discussant behaviours, such as by saying, thank you to participants who respond effectively online, can be helpful to encourage courtesy and interaction.
Don't ignore bad behaviour	Request change (privately) in poor discussant behaviours and have a written netiquette statement to refer to.

Expect flames to occur   Participants may breach etiquette and respond with harsh or vulgar language. If this problem should occur, the facilitator needs to react and remind people (privately) about computer etiquette.

Be responsive   Respond quickly to each contribution. One way of doing this is by posting a personal message to the contributor or by referring to the author's comments in a post to the conference. In some conferences, it is not advisable to respond to each individual contribution, but better to respond to several at once by weaving them together.

Provide for administration   Provide information about activities for such things as ezine registration, purchasing and other administrative functions often.

Procedural leadership   The facilitator should initiate procedures and stifle frustrating procedural discussions. Change what isn't working, but don't allow the conference to be taken over by discussion of failed procedure rather than content or more useful discussion.

Be clear   Clearly state the conference topic and the expectations for participants within the conference. Clarify the topic and expectations throughout the conference proceedings.

Promote peer learning   Encourage novice email or e-conference users to work with more experienced peers.

Avoid lecturing   Single contributions should be limited to no more than two screens. Longer postings are hard to read on screen, become tedious, and impede discussion.

Giving direction   It is important not to give too much direction. Participants will often rebel if the structural design of the conference is excessive.

Provide time to learn   Provide adequate time for novice users to be comfortable with the technology before they must participate.

Don't overload   The facilitator should pace the conference so that the equivalent of about one long post per day is made. If the participants have a lot to contribute, the moderator should contribute less so that the slower participants can keep up.

Handle tangents appropriately	Return inappropriate digressions to the author or guide the participants back to the original topic.
Vary participants' contribution	If there is a participant who appears overly outspoken, ask that person (privately) to wait a few responses before contributing. Similarly, ask less outspoken individuals to participate more actively.
Comments on metacommunications	Request metacommunications by inviting participants to tell how they feel about the course within the conference.
Synchronise and resynchronise	As much as possible, ensure that all participants begin in unison and in an organised fashion.
Informality	Depending upon the instructional objectives of the course, the facilitator may decide that informality should be encouraged. One way to stress the informality of this communications medium is to let people know that perfect grammar and typing are much less important than making their meaning clear.
Use technical support	It may be useful to have technical support people available to answer emailed or telephoned inquiries. Before the conference begins, the facilitator should know who is available for technical support that is needed beyond his/her skills level.
End the sessions	Decisively end each discussion thread and the conference. Conclude discussions so that they don't drag on after they have served their purpose.

Newsgroups

A great way to generate traffic on your web site or to sell directly to the internet community is by posting selected messages in appropriate Usenet Newsgroups. These are basically discussion groups for individuals with a specific interest. There are over 100,000 different Newsgroups on the internet so there will almost definitely be some which contain your potential customers. The first step is to make a list of the Newsgroups you feel are appropriate for your posting. On the web, advertising is accepted and expected. On Newsgroups it is not. This is one area where a very good understanding of Netiquette is required but the rewards can be worth it.

Business related newsgroups could be a good way of internet marketing and can present a great opportunity to increase traffic to your website through participation and advertising. The problem is, people rarely appreciate advertising on their favourite newsgroups or pay attention to signatures at the end of participants' messages. Being perceived as a spammer can really hurt your website's reputation, so how can you get the most out of this popular medium? Participate in newsgroups and discussion lists which deal with the subject of your website. By including your marketing signature you can subtly advertise your company and attract traffic interested in your site's content. These visitors will be more likely to buy your products or services or click on your banner advertisements than visitors responding to an advertisement.

Promoting your website in newsgroups can take a lot preparatory research, but it's often worth the time. Be sure to post only to groups with related content which are frequented by the sort of people you want to visit your website and who accept advertising. Always include your full URL in your postings, without punctuation. Punctuation will add itself to your link, ensuring people who click on it will receive a '404 Page Not Found' error.

A discussion list is like bulletin board post sent to your email box. It doesn't require that subscribers visit your website (which is somewhat of a disadvantage if you want to sell stuff on your website). The advantage is that once someone subscribes, they're likely to stick around longer. If you decide to start a discussion list, look for directories to submit it to and always include a message in the footer referring subscribers back to your website.

Some participation tips include:

- Read the FAQ. It should be listed regularly on the newsgroup and archived somewhere. Check Dejanews **www.dejanews.com** if you don't see it after a week or so.
- Some marketers suggest posting regularly. What they don't say is that if you do, you need to post a different message. People will get annoyed if they repeatedly see the same message. If they didn't respond the first time, they certainly won't when they see it again.
- If you can come up with new reasons for people to visit your website, post one every few weeks, or once a month. Preferably include announcements of new content, new subjects, new ezines or discussion

lists you are starting, or significant changes in the presentation of your website.

- Check what sort of messages are posted to the newsgroup, and how many there are. Don't advertise on newsgroups, which consist entirely of advertisements, or newsgroups with no postings.
- Be sure to tailor your marketing message to the list it will appear on. People will be less angry (and more likely to respond) if your message speaks directly to them, answering their needs.
- Don't list a message simultaneously on multiple newsgroups. Yes, it's faster, but the more newsgroups you send copies to, the more you look like a spammer.
- Don't ignore a discussion list or newsgroup because it is moderated. Check the rules for submission, and email the moderator with your marketing message, including the reasons you think their audience will benefit from the message and how it pertains to their topic. If your message is posted, it will receive a better response than on unmoderated groups.
- Only post advertisements to newsgroups which have a topic related to your website, or are of significant interest to your target audience.
- Make sure your marketing messages include your website address and a reason for people to visit. Tell people what you want them to do: visit your website, bookmark it, and/or tell others about it. Make sure you type the full URL – www.yourdomain.com – without punctuation. Punctuation usually breaks your link.

Choose the newsgroups lists you participate in carefully. They should be interesting and informative to you, and give you the opportunity to show off your expertise.

9

International Marketing

```
┌─────────────────────────────────────────────┐
│              CLICK-ONS                        │
│            Europe online                      │
│      Marketing in another language            │
│     Budgeting for an international site        │
│        Marketing a web brand abroad           │
│  Factors influencing product usage by country │
│        International search engines            │
│         International website design           │
│        Where to look for information           │
└─────────────────────────────────────────────┘
```

Key reasons why you should give attention to using your company's website to reach out to global markets:

☑ Expand internationally before your competitors do. Those who get in first have a 'first mover advantage', early recognition that helps them gain later market acceptance.

☑ People in other countries do not find that much content in their own language, and are hungry for websites that bring them what they want.

☑ Satisfy your shareholders: companies who have established global sales have a higher value than strictly domestic companies

Global depends on local

Every company that markets primarily through a web site is technically global. However, if a UK-based, web-centered company is to get truly significant traffic and do significant e-commerce in another country, it will almost certainly need a physical presence in that country. Only through a physical presence can a web company seriously promote and market its site in the country, support the site with PR, and handle language, legal, tax and fulfillment issues.

Portability

Does your product or service travel well? Learn from the experience of firms that have preceded you on the web. They've found it easier to establish a value proposition for products or services at the core of the internet economy, such as retailing, travel and leisure, entertainment, and financial services, than for other verticals. Establish whether a given product or service has any appeal outside your traditional markets without being redeveloped, re-engineered, repackaged, or run through rigorous market or safety certification tests. Use this subset of your catalogue to determine trends, understand market needs, and begin to build your presence and brand in international markets. Align products and services with market needs and opportunities and validate your choices with local knowledge. Once you've identified a particular product or service that could do well in a given country, engage the services of your local staff or a consultant with local knowledge who can perform a sanity check on your decision. Once you have your candidate products in hand, check out the regulatory and logistical landscape in the countries where you'd like to sell them.

European and Asian businesses have a natural advantage when approaching the multi-linguality of the internet as they have much more experience selling in a trans-border, trans-culture environment.

eMarketer, 'The eBusiness Report,' December 1999

Can people buy what you're selling? Three factors are critical as you look for the next demographically correct country to target. First is there a large enough population online? For example, Brazil might look like a less desirable market if you consider nothing but percentage of the population online. However, once you exclude rural areas and the rain forest, focusing instead on the densely populated cities along the Atlantic coast, Brazil becomes a much more attractive online market. Studies, such as 'Risk E-Business: Seizing the Opportunity of Global E-Readiness' (**www.mcconnellinternational.com**), provide a road map for evaluating whether a market has the requisite infrastructure to support profitable e-commerce.

Second is buyer demographics. Do consumers online have enough disposable income to buy what you want to sell them? Lastly is means of payment. The ability to pay according to local terms and conditions is critical. If your online transaction depends on the customer typing in his American Express card number, you'll find high numbers of abandoned shopping carts in countries like Germany with low credit card penetration. International online merchants must arrange for alternate payment means, such as credit cards like Japan's JCB.

E-Commerce Sales in 2003 by Region

US	$ 284 Billion	39%
Asia-Pacific	$ 992 billion	14%
Europe	$ 3,200 billion	32%
Latin America	$ 124 billion	2%
Other	$ 949 billion	13%
TOTAL	**$ 7,300 billion**	

Source: The Gartner Group

Europe online

Some stats and facts:
- Europe's network-service providers are committing large scale finance to broadband.
- Not only are most European countries going online at an unprecedented rate, but 15 countries of the European Union are now accepting a common currency (the euro). The euro is already legal tender between

banks for company payments, and the banknotes and coins of each member country will disappear by mid-2002. The combination of these two factors is widely thought to give strong stimulation to e-commerce, and projections are for $200-220 bn in European e-commerce in 2002.

- London has surpassed New York as the world's busiest exchange for internet traffic.

- E-commerce presents the prospect of an economic, rather policy-based, push toward expanding the scope and volume of Pan-European business activity. At the same time, the companies leading the march in European B2B are likely to be globally familiar names, says Andrew Parker, an Amsterdam-based senior analyst for Forrester Research. 'Both in B2B and B2C, Forrester believes that established businesses have the upper hand in European e-commerce. I believe the most important development will be the emergence of online-market leaders from among Europe's large businesses – companies that will have the same status in European Internet lore as Cisco, Yahoo, and Amazon have had in the US,' Parker says. 'No one has that status today, but companies like Deutsche Bank, with its Moneyshelf (an internet portal for managing personal finances) consumer offering, along with companies such as Shell and Nokia in broader Internet activity, have the potential to emerge as exemplary innovators (in creating effective e-commerce business models).'

- ISPs in the UK and elsewhere in Europe continue to wrangle over how to charge consumers for internet access. Free internet access often requires users to pay for local phone calls that, in most of Europe, are metered. As Pascal Dormal, strategy and business development director for Belgian telecommunications firm Telenet says, 'The free internet is not free if you have to pay for metered calling. It means that people stay online as little as possible.' Europe's free-access ISPs generate revenues through advertising and sharing phone tolls with their network providers. These are usually old, state-monopoly phone companies, which, years after privatisation and deregulation began, are still in the process of 'unbundling the local loop' to give competitors cheaper and easier access to customers. In Germany, France, and Spain, these former monopolies also own their countries' most popular ISPs.

Examples of virtual stores throughout Europe

Here are some examples of good sources for European online shopping, all with secure payment systems:

Multilingual Shopping Sites

- Hotwin (**www.hotwin.com/hotwin**), a database of European e-commerce sites.

France

A French marketing research company, Motivaction (**www.enquete. motivaction.fr**) made a comparative study of 5,000 French people online and their online buying habits. 44% of them have seen an online merchant, and 40% have already bought something online. Of those who have bought online, 80% said that they paid by sending their credit card number via the net. What do the French buy? 40% of those interviewed had bought software, 27% books, 22% CD-ROM, 22% computer equipment, and 18% audio CDs. The survey also asked them what they wanted to see developed, and they replied theatres tickets (50%), travel tickets (46%), banking services (33%), and publication subscriptions (33%). Some French e-commerce sites to visit include:

- BuyCentral (**www.buycentral.com/fr/index.html**) a guide of e-commerce in France.
- Web Merchant (**www.web-merchant.com**) a database of French e-commerce sites.
- 123Achat (**www.123achat.com**) references over 600 French-language commerce sites, giving indications such as currencies, payment method accepted, security level or delivery time.
- A sampling of French e-commerce sites can be seen at **www.glreach.com/gbc/fr/shopping.php3**. If you read French, the latest news about ecommerce in France is available at **www.ebusiness.org** and **internet-marchand.com**.

Germany

- ZD reports that 57% of German surfers have already bought something online. Horizont reports that e-commerce in Germany will triple in the next two years. (Source: Horizont).
- The German shopping search engine is called Shop.de (**www.shop.de**) complete with 15,000 shops in the database.
- Shop24 (**www.shopping24.de**), Germany's largest shopping mall (1.5 million articles).
- Netzmarkt (**www.netzmarkt.de**), top German online shopping mall.
- Stern Magazine (Germany's equivalent to 'Life Magazine') offers a Shopping Guide (**www.stern.de:1814/shop**) of many German online stores, and rates them with stars.

- A sampling of German e-commerce sites can be seen at **www.glreach .com/gbc/de/shopping.php3**.

Italy
- Magellano E-Shop (**www.shop.smau.it**) offers over 150 products, representing 50 different manufacturers. Though offering a wide range of products, E-Shop's primary line consists of computer software and hardware. All purchases are made through major credit cards, using the Telepay electronic system.

Sweden
- Boxman (**www.boxman.com**), Europe's answer to Amazon (online bookstore), available in all Scandinavian languages, Finnish and English.

Eastern Europe
- The Ozone Electronic Bookstore (**www.03.ru**), the most successful Russian e-commerce business.

Outside of Europe

Latin America
- Cadê?/Ibope Research in Brazil published a study of Brazilian ecommerce, finding that 19% of Brazilian internet users have already shopped on the net and another 62% showed interest on buying through the net in the future, thus showing the potencial for e-commerce in Brazil. 72% of the users declared to possess a credit card, 52% of which were bearers of international credit cards.
- AOL launched operations in Latin America in December 1998, and they said this in their press release about this launch: 'The middle class is 100 million people and it's growing by 10 million a year. The middle class has a gross national product higher than Germany. There are a lot of people with money. They control 65% of the wealth and have the power of consumption, even in a recession. There is enormous value in the marketplace.' (**www.techweb.com/wire/story/TWB19981216S0012**)

Brazil
- Universo Online (Brazil's biggest ISP, content provider and web developer group – (**http://cdf.uol.com.br**) includes a virtual mall featuring 26 stores and companies: flowers, compact disks, books, and clothing are sold, as well as PCs. They operate in Brazil as well as other countries in Latin America.

Payment mechanisms

Ways for a virtual shop to collect moneys online <u>in UK</u>:

- Emporia: **www.emporia.net**.
- NetBanx: **www.netbanx.com** and **www.netinvest.co.uk**. Provides connection to processing network in the UK. Allows merchants to transact in 116 currencies and settle in 16. Set-up charges are between £75-£500 depending upon the complexity of the service. Commission on sales depends upon the volume of monthly sales. Less than £2,000 is 4%, going down to 1% after sales of £10,000 per month.
- DataCash: **www.datacash.com** (officially approved by and connected permanently to the following acquiring banks: NatWest Streamline, Girobank, American Express, Barclays Merchant Services, Royal Bank of Scotland). UK merchants using DataCash are able to trade in more than 150 currencies and to have the funds credited to their account in one of 16 currencies (settled).
- CyberSource: **www.cybersource.com** is a US company with partnership relationships that allow it to provide many services to countries outside the US. Some of the services they provide include the ability to transact business in 28 currencies including the euro. £295 per month is minimum invoice for their fees, that pays for about 300 to 400 transactions per month at UK 90p (US$1.45 per transaction).

Ways for a virtual shop to collect moneys online in <u>Germany</u>:

- E-cash software was put into action last October by Deutsche Bank (Germany's largest bank: **www.deutsche-bank.de**). Many German people do not use cheques and credit cards to pay for merchandise or services they purchase; they use bank transfers instead. E-cash had to devise a secure method for customers to fill out a form on a web page, which debits their bank account for the amount of the purchase. This is the only such application for debit payments in Germany.
- A recent survey of people online in Germany and Austria showed that 40% of those surveyed have already bought something online. Most popular was the automobile/motorcycle/sport area (16%), followed by the computer area (15%). (source: Global Online magazine).

Ways for a virtual shop to collect moneys online in <u>France</u>:

- France Telecom offers a web-based E-Business solution that was developed by Open Market, called TeleCommerce (**www.francetelecom.**

fr/vanglais/actualite/actu.htm), in association with banks BNP and Credit Agricole. It goes much further than other solutions, as it does not require users to input their credit card numbers, since they already have given their credit card details the first time they bought on a Telecommerce merchant. $2,500 installation cost, plus $150 per month and 3% of transactions. Since France Telecom has vast experience in setting up virtual stores in their 17 years of Minitel experience, this should prove to be a success, as it carries the credibility of one of the national telecom operators. It has been installed first for Le Marche de la France, a virtual shopping mall of French luxury products. TeleCommerce is a complete buying system with a virtual basket, commands management, automatic calculation of VAT, tips, customs rights and statistics. Since France Telecom has already been quite successful with the same sort of virtual shops for its Minitel (which contains today 25,000 virtual shops), this web development is simply the next logical step. What makes it unusual is that the web visitor does not have to give his or her credit card number to the merchant: TeleCommerce is responsible for this. The customer can shop in various shops and not have to fill out the payment and delivery form each time.

- Kleline software (**www.kleline.fr**) is the French leader in e-cash (similar to Digicash). which offers both a 'virtual wallet' that resides on one's hard disk (for sums less than 100 FF = $17), and regular secured payment for more than $17. They are a tad expensive at $2,500 for a license, plus $5,000 for setup and installation, plus 3% of transaction costs. Online shoppers can pay for their purchases in 20 different currencies. Kleline is currently testing the 'millicent' feature (for spending very small amounts). Virtual shopping centers that have chosen Kleline's software for payment mechanism include Globe Online (**www.globeonline.fr**), Trios Suisses (**www.trios-suisses.fr**, a large French mail-order store).

- Payline (**www.sg2.fr/decouvri/domint/teleserv/payline/sg2-payline. html**) is promoting itself as the top payment solution on the Internet in France for virtual store, costing a monthly fee, plus setup charges.

- SIPS (**www.atos-group.com/sips**), which handles back-office work and can even work with multiple languages and currencies.

- The first French bank to get into the secure payment business was Credit Mutuel (**www.creditmutuel.fr**). Their lower price has permitted them to attract more clients than the other solution (around 200 in France): a merchant pays a monthly fee and each transaction is charged a % of the transaction.

Ways for a virtual shop to collect moneys online in <u>Switzerland</u>:

- Computer World GmbH has launched a service for Swiss companies to sell online (**www.swisskaufhaus.ch**)). For a setup fee and monthly fee, they will host a Swiss company's website and provide the backend services to collect credit card purchases.

Ways for a virtual shop to collect moneys online elsewhere in <u>Europe</u>:

- Finland: UUnet is working with Merita Bank to provide e-commerce.
- Norway: The Norske Bank provides a platform for e-commerce.
- Austria: Bank Austria provides a platform for e-commerce.

On-line banking in Europe is starting to take off. Non-traditional banks are taking advantage of the tremendous cost savings realizable from on-line banking. Leading banks includes:

<u>Country</u>	<u>Name</u>	<u>URL</u>
UK	First Direct Bank	**www.firstdirect.co.uk**
Germany	Allgemeine Deutsche Direktbank	**www.direktbank.de**
	Bank 24 (Deutsche Bank)	**www.bank24.de**
	Santander Direkt Bank	**www.santander.de**
Spain	Banco Direct	
France	Cortal	**www.banque-cortal.fr**
	Banque Directe	**www.banquedirecte.com**

A key driving force is the cost of banking on-line versus banking by telephone or by teller. Bank 24 of Germany estimates the on-line cost per transaction at $0.01 versus $1.12 by telephone, and double that amount in person. With the transition to the euro, which became fully implemented in 11 EU countries on 1 January 2002, on-line banks will be well positioned to offer European-wide on-line banking services, by taking advantage of economies of scale and the lack of need of physical bank branches.

Marketing in another language

Today more than half the internet users in the world have a mother tongue other than English. According to estimates, that number will increase to 70 percent within two years. By contrast, more than two-thirds of web pages are currently in English. Japanese and German are in second position with almost 6 percent each. It is almost certain that an increasing percentage of the new sites launched on the web in the next two years will be in languages other than English. Chinese languages are poised for especially strong growth. Also, an increasing number of companies will make their current English-language sites available in several other languages. However, the web will continue to contribute toward English becoming a more globally used language.

> A number of web sites provide, at no cost, some good information about the language of the web (Global Reach **www.euromktg. com/globstats/index.php3**).

What is involved in taking an English-language web site and developing, for example, a German equivalent? At one end of the spectrum, if you literally translated the site word for word it would be disastrous. At a minimum, the words need to be adapted into the current usage and colloquialisms of the country. A native of the country who currently lives in the country is essential for performing this task adequately. More important to consider is whether all of the site content is even relevant in Germany. Somewhere between a direct translation and a total remake of the site is usually what is needed.

How much priority should you place on developing your site in other languages, as opposed to perfecting your English-language version? At a minimum, when you establish a physical presence in a country and begin your marketing efforts, it is mandatory to offer your site in the primary language of the country. When you enter France, you must offer your site in French! But what about a country like Canada, where a quarter of the population has French as its primary language and a smaller percentage is, at the least, uncomfortable with English? Most major sites that originated in Canada and are targeted at Canadian consumers offer a choice of English or French.

While it is not necessary to translate your entire web site into a number of languages, you really should consider translating at least the most important pages. When you market to countries where English is spoken well, e.g. Holland and Scandinavia, remember that people in these countries don't particularly read English sites, just because they can read English. They read their local news and web sites in their local language. If English comes up, it's no problem as it would be in Southern Europe, but advertisers in their local magazines certainly do not market to them in English. The local language is used. So do not think that you don't have to make an effort to localise in these countries, just because they read English.

Remember that you can 'fold in' languages over time, so that you start with, say, two languages, gradually develop those, while planting the seeds of other languages. Do part of it at a time, and increase the marketing efforts on the language sections that you feel most confident with. This is where your first overseas sales will probably start: where you have put in the necessary work to make your localised web site credible in that country.

Whether or not a person speaks English has nothing to do with the responsibility of a website to communicate in the language of the target markets. Dutch, Danes and Swedes read English well and yet they surf in their own language. They live their life in their own language, not in English. If you want to attract their attention, your site has to go where they are, that is, use online marketing techniques in their own language.

'Marketing always takes place in the language of the target market.'

Canadian and Swiss aren't languages, but rather names for the denizens of Canada and Switzerland. Therein lies the problem. There are 246 internet domains in the world, each representing a political entity such as Japan, Canada, and Switzerland. From an internet perspective, the political entity must combine with language and culture to create a distinct market. Consider:

- Canada is a multicultural country where English and French are the official languages. Total: provincial variation aside, these two linguistic markets, plus a growing population of Mandarin speakers in Vancouver and Toronto, mean that Canada actually comprises *three* markets.
- Switzerland has three major linguistic populations: French, German, and Italian plus a splinter group of Romansch speakers. Total: *three* or *four* markets, depending on the commercial reach of Romansch.
- Japan is a homogeneous market where everyone speaks Japanese. Total: *one* market.

Outside the seven countries where English is native, and India too, there is no form of marketing in any country that happens in English. People live their life in their own language, and your marketing needs to follow, whether the media is newspaper/magazine ads/articles, radio/TV, billboards or websites. English is not understood well in Germany. Not in Japan. And certain not in Southern European countries, South America or China. If a website is selling IT products, English is usually sufficient, after an initial page in the language of the target market (a 'jumper page') is available. IT people worldwide have to be conversant in English, but the initial attraction of their attention has to happen in their own language. But for other services/products, the deeper into the population one goes, the more translation is necessary.

Europeans have been engaged in multi-cultural marketing for centuries, and it is natural to them. And today, nearly one-half of their corporate sites are multilingual. If you have competitors who are more serious about the world market than you are, you will gradually lose ground to these competitors.

If these arguments have convinced you to develop a multilingual site, you can start with just one page, or a few important pages, in the languages of important target markets. To learn which languages are most represented on the internet, look at the chart on **www.glreach.com/globstats**. Over time, it will be clear which languages are most important, and more of the website can be translated. It is fine to start with just a few pages that lead back into the English part of the site. But you could run the risk that someone who is interested after a few clicks, and then comes to an English page, and gets lost among other English pages, will simply click elsewhere. It is all too easy for a web visitor to leave the site if he/she does not understand English well.

Language creates potential barriers to the international sale of products on a number of fronts. If you decide to aggressively market your product in Italy, your marketing efforts will obviously have to be in the Italian language. It's also obvious that if you are going to try to repeat the success you have had in the UK with your best-selling book 'Toe Nail Clipping for Experts' by marketing it in Germany, you will have to translate and adapt the book for the German market. Less obvious is that if you decide to market your umbrellas in Canada, you will have to offer the product in dual-language (English and French) packaging. Moreover, the product you sell in your home market will require language adjustments before you can market it in another country.

Here are two pitfalls to avoid when it comes to translation:

- Do not assume that a translation agency is sufficient to help your company go global. Nor is an international marketing consultancy sufficient for this purpose, or a legal firm or for that matter, any one piece of the whole picture. You will need all these elements working together to go global.

- Do not assume that 'they speak English in other countries, so there is no reason to translate our marketing materials or website'. Even if some Europeans can read English, they have a tendency to ignore advertising in English. Many times they assume that if a company does not advertise in their own language, they would not want to buy from that company. Willy Brandt, the former German chancellor, put it this way: 'If I'm selling to you, I speak your language. If I'm buying, dann müssen Sie Deutsch sprechen (then you must speak German).'

Today, English is the 'lingua franca' of the internet - 78 percent of all websites and 96 percent of eCommerce sites are in English. Yet by 2002, more than half of net users will speak a language other than English and by 2003, it is predicted that the majority of web content will be in a language other than English.

eMarketer, 'The eBusiness Report,' December 1999

Content optimisation tips

It's a good idea to invest in software that identifies the country your visitors are coming from, then automatically serves up a home page in that language with a text link to secondary language choices. Translate at least three to five pages of your site for each non-English-speaking country in your target market. It used to be that you could get by with translating just one page, but you need more now to get indexed by the robot engines.

Site translations

To be listed on any foreign search engine, you must have a foreign translation of your site and a foreign domain name. Translate at least five to six pages deep, because one or two pages are not enough to be picked up by foreign crawlers. Literal translations can be unintentionally laughable or insulting for instance, it's important not to translate all the internet-specific words, such as 'browser,' 'page,' 'impression,' and 'visit,' because these often remain in English. The best translations are done through local, nonautomated translation services.

One of the leaders in machine translation is Lernout & Houspie (**www.lhs.be**), who is developing a speech-driven front-end and back-end, whereby you can speak to the net access device, and someone else understands what you say, spoken to them in their own language. It's simply a matter of combining speech-recognition technology and automatic translation. Hire a translator for web pages, but use machine translation (or combination of that with human management) in email correspondence. Machine translation, as it is called, works by identifying the source language text and using a set of language rules plus a huge vocabulary database to come up with the best translation for text. Sentences are translated in accordance with their full context.

Budgeting for an international site

In budgeting for a multilingual web site, place at least twice as much budget into the promotion of the site as in its creation. After you have determined the amount to be budgeted for its promotion, delimit the number of language zones that will be targeted initially. Apportion the total budget according to the percentages. For example, if a site wants to target German, French and Spanish-speaking countries, a simple analysis shows this many people are online in these countries (April, 2000 figures):

German	20 million
French	13 million
Spanish	20 million
TOTAL:	53 million in the combined target markets

A logical place to start would be to put 38 percent of the international online marketing budget into German and Spanish promotion and 24 percent into French promotion. Next, decide which techniques of web promotion are best to use for the kind of product or service you are selling, e.g. search engine optimisation. That gives an immediate incentive to click on it. Another efficient tactic is online guerrilla marketing, which includes asking for strategic links from synergistic sites in other countries, and working the email discussion groups and Newsgroups of a particular subject in the target country markets.

Marketing a web brand abroad

When you launch your web business in your own country, you probably will take the traditional steps to develop a business plan, one of which is creating the marketing plan. You are likely to conduct thorough research of the market for your product or service to find out the size of the market and the demographics of primary user groups, map the competitive situation, determine your position in the market, determine a shipping-and-handling strategy, set five-year sales/revenue targets and established budgets, develop a brand name, and hired advertising and public relations agencies. With all these pieces in place, hopefully you will achieve a successful launch in your own country. Now you plan to market your web business in other countries.

Markets with the highest concentration of online population:

38.64	million Japanese speakers
27.5	million German speakers
18.9	million Spanish speakers (US Hispanic, Spain, and Latin America)
40.7	million Chinese speakers
16.6	million French speakers (Quebec, France, Switzerland and Belgium)
9.6	million Dutch speakers
11.5	million Portuguese speakers (Brazil included)

Write a new marketing plan for each country

All the work that you did to develop your marketing plan in your own country needs to be done from scratch when you plan to market your web venture in another country. This means researching the market for each country. Don't simply use the size of a country's population to project the potential market size. If 20 percent of your country's adult population purchases at least one book a month, in another country the figure could be 2 percent or 40 percent. Don't assume that the competitive share of the market is similar in every country. Even shipping-and-handling issues are not consistent around the world.

If you use traditional media to market your web site, you may need to use a very different media mix in other countries. We may live in a global village, but media habits do vary from country to country. Most advertising and PR agencies are now either global or have global affiliations. It will likely be beneficial to your business to use global agencies; that should result in a more consistent presentation of your brand image around the world.

For insightful papers on the subject, visit Emerald, where you will find the International Marketing Review.

(**www.emeraldinsight.com/imr.html**)

Localise

The Gartner Group predicts that by 2004 the European internet economy alone will be worth $1 trillion. But what works in one country is definitely not guaranteed to work in another. Market researcher IDC and globalisation consulting firm eTranslate teamed up recently to survey 30,000 web users in 27 countries about their e-commerce preferences. The result: Localise! While many consider English a universal language, even in Sweden and Denmark, countries with a high degree of English proficiency, 64% and 63%, respectively, users prefer their own language.

Preference for language other than English

Country	%
China	85
Japan	84
Brazil	82
Spain	82
Argentina	81
Peru	81
Germany	79
Korea	75
Venezuela	74
Columbia	71

Least willing to buy across borders

US	9
China	21
Germany	28
Sweden	36
UK	37

Most willing to buy across borders

Chile	76

Venezuela	76
Puerto Rico	75
Malaysia	74
Peru	72

Source: Sep. 2000 IDC

Considering the linguistic and cultural variation within a single country, the question becomes 'Which market first?' instead of 'Which country first?' In some cases, it may make sense to target only one of the markets within a country, national laws permitting. Most UK and US companies first pursue the English-speaking markets. Then they might move on to countries in Western Europe. Over time, more adventurous companies add local language content and country-specific logistics. While this incremental approach is safe, it leaves openings for faster-moving local competitors to move in, or for your traditional rivals who might move faster and invest more money to jump ahead for international markets.

Where localisation was being used, it should be extended beyond just language. eCommerce firms are advised to carry localisation throughout the entire buying process. Firms should offer product selections that combine local taste, original editorial content, local payment methods, and customer service.

Torris, Dr. Therese, Forrester Research,
'The Best of Europe's eCommerce,' August 1999

Select a strong international brand name

A commonly quoted example of a brand name that worked well in North America but was problematic in certain other countries was the Chevy Nova; 'no va' in Spanish means 'doesn't go.' Many companies choose a brand name that is a fabricated word, such as Xerox, because it is internationally applicable and country neutral. However, before you finalise your brand name, check thoroughly for its implications in major countries and cultures around the world.

Marketing a web brand in multiple countries

When you launched your e-commerce business in your own country, you may not have considered that the products or services you are selling to your home market may be totally non-functional, or at least unsuitable, in most countries of the world. The nonfunctionality or unsuitability of your products or services outside your home market can relate to electric power specifications, electric outlets, language, or legislation, among many other reasons.

> The majority of internet users speak a primary language other than English, so companies that offer opt-in-list rentals must carefully address the preferred language for each person.

Virtual overseas offices

When you sell internationally, it is best to give the customers the choice of how they want to contact you. Besides email, there are other basic means to attract more prospects and customers. There is a lot to be said for the concept of 'virtual offices' abroad, whereby your company has a phone number in important cities that doubles as a voicemail/fax contact point local to the prospect/customer.

Once you are convinced to make an action plan to expand internationally, you will need to locate firms to assist you in all the various aspects about globalizing your business, e.g. marketing consultants, lawyers, freight forwarders, after-sales support teams, etc. How do you find knowledgeable partners to navigate through the myriad details needed to globalize your business and minimise the risk of investment? When looking for advice, here are several questions to ask them:

? Do you have staff on the spot in countries my company wants to target? Local people?

? Are you easy to reach by phone and by email?

? What can be done in local marketing, both online and offline, to make my company be taken seriously?

? What telecom services and call centres are available, to centralise marketing and after-sales support in the language of the markets?

? What legal structure does my company need in order to be able to sell in these countries?

Worldwide internet usage near 430 million

More than 429 million people worldwide have internet access, with the US and Canada accounting for 41 percent of the figure. A 'First Quarter 2001 Global Internet Trends' report released from Nielsen//NetRatings found that Europe, the Middle East and Africa has the second-highest proportion of access with 27 percent, Asia Pacific has 20 percent online and 4 percent of the population of Latin America has access to the internet. 'Don't expect this American domination to last long, though,' said Richard Goosey, chief of measurement science and analytics for ACNielsen eRatings.com. 'Compared to a year ago, significantly more households in Europe and Asia Pacific now have a PC in the home and a greater proportion of homes are making use of that PC to connect to the internet. Over the next 12 months, another 9 percent of European households and 12 percent of Asia Pacific households plan on acquiring internet access.'

Legislation

Although some product categories are not heavily legislated, others are, and the legislation can be very different in each country. Product categories that can involve a minefield of marketing regulations include tobacco, alcohol, drugs, firearms, and any products that involve children. Once again, the product you have so successfully marketed in your own country may require serious re-engineering before it can be marketed in other countries.

In a recent Forrester report, The Best of Europe's eCommerce, they assert, 'Localisation is indispensable for attracting large numbers of customers in Europe's fragmented market. Even customers who speak English prefer sites that offer their local language as well as local product selections, relevant payment options, and localised versions of customer service.'

Torris, Dr. Therese, Forrester Research,
'The Best of Europe's eCommerce,' August 1999

Consider the national laws and regulations. Your site has to deal with laws that regulate how your product or service works, how you sell it, and the tariffs, taxes, privacy laws, and other minutiae that affect its sale in a given market. Informational sites maintained by the Chamber of Commerce in your target countries, and the European Union (**www.europa.eu.int**) can give you some basic advice on getting started. Sites can provide some insight on the privacy laws in other countries. You also need to consider international logistics. Remember: you've got to deliver goods to international customers and deal with post-sales service, including physical product returns. Local business practices must also be taken into account. Less obvious than national laws and tough logistics is the way of doing business in a given country. For example, the Korean *chaebol* and Japanese *keiretsu* (these are vertically integrated, expansive conglomerates) are few in number, but they control the means of distribution in those two countries. To compete effectively in Korea and Japan, you may have to align yourself with the most appropriate group.

Things such as copyright and trade regulations can inhibit doing business overseas. One of the toughest issues is the variation and fluctuation of international tax rules. Commercial tax rates vary from country to country. Tax rates change frequently too. And then, besides knowing the current rates by locale, you have to know them by product or service. When you're doing business overseas, you usually have to pay taxes at each step along the value-added chain. For example, all Euro countries impose a VAT, or value-added tax, on all products and many services produced in their country.

Asian/Pacific online ad market growing

Despite current negative market sentiment surrounding the internet economy in Asia/Pacific, online advertising is forecasted to see solid year-on-year growth, according to a recent study by research company IDC. The report found that there has been an overall increase in online advertising spending by traditional companies, while online advertising spending by dot-coms is all but dead. The report reveals that online advertising in Asia/Pacific (excluding Japan) accounted for a little more than 0.5 percent of total advertising revenue in the region during 2000. In addition, the amount of revenue generated by dot-com's online advertising decreased by 34 percent between 1999 and 2000, and was forecasted to drop by another 51 percent in 2001. Looking forward, online advertising in Asia/Pacific is expected to grow from $225 million in 2001 to $702 million in 2004, with a compounded annual growth rate of 46 percent. China is expected to be one of the fastest growing regions in terms of year-on-year growth, while countries such as Korea and Taiwan will need to combat declining CPM rates in order to pull ahead. IDC found that across the board, all countries were experiencing a slow-down in advertising bookings, but the market is expected to correct itself as more traditional companies begin advertising online.

Factors influencing product usage by country

Three key factors which determine the purchase and consumption of products by the populations of different countries:

- There are historical and cultural differences of product consumption by country. We all know how much the British love a good cuppa, while for Americans the day starts only after the first cup of coffee.
- Geographic location can have an impact on a person's product needs. For example, air conditioning is less important in a cold or temperate climate. And a bicycle is a practical form of transportation in a very dense urban community, but less so in wide-open rural farmlands.
- The financial prosperity of the inhabitants of a country is important. Russians probably have as great a need and desire to own a car as Americans do, but because of the different levels of prosperity in the two countries, automobile ownership is much higher in the USA.

An example of different product usage within a country

Global wine consumption: France and Italy are in second and third place respectively, when it comes to enjoying a glass of wine (Luxembourg is first), with about 60 litres consumed annually per capita. The population of the US drinks less wine than all the European countries, at just 7 litres per capita, but is still very far ahead of Japan at 1.7 litres. Consumption differences of this magnitude underline why it is essential to analyse the market for your product by country at a very early stage in your business planning process and not to project sales volumes from one country to another.

International search engines

Non-English-speaking populations prefer to be addressed in their native languages, even if they understand English. And when it comes to search engines, these people are more likely to use search engines in their own language. Fortunately, many people in other countries have learned to search the internet using American-based engines, such as Google, Yahoo!, and Lycos. The best place to start is with Open Directory Project (ODP – **http://dmoz.org**), because you can find all sorts of non-American directories there. ODP also has many regional sites.

As the rest of the world wakes up to doing business over the internet, the US online numbers reassesses its own domestic market, given that it represents only 4% of the world's population and 20% of the world's economy. Jupiter's Globalisation Report, published in January 2001, finds that the US share of the global internet population will drop from 36% today to approximately 24% in 2005.

Registration in the international indexes

Getting listed on directories and search engines is the most logical and cost-effective means to placing your site where potential visitors start their searches on the internet. When web users outside of English-speaking countries search for something on the web, they search in their native language. You can make it easy for them to find your site by listing your web site in these international indexes. But in order to register a web page in a non-English index, it has to appear in the language of that index. If your site is not available in other languages, the solution here is to use a one-page summary of your web site, translated into the languages of your target markets. Besides translating your product/service description, be sure to translate descriptive statements, keywords, and categories, so that overseas visitors to your site can find it in their own language. Certain indexes require you to have an address (both postal and server addresses) in their country, in order to have a listing. After completing an index registration, it can take up to 4 to 6 weeks in some busy indexes for your web site to appear. Check up on each index regularly, the first time some 4-6 weeks after the initial index registrations, then every 3-6 months thereafter.

France

Voila	www.voila.fr//?refresh
Yahoo! France	http://fr.yahoo.com
MSN France	http://search2.msn.fr
Nomade.fr	www.nomade.fr
Lycos France	www.lycos.fr
LookSmart France	www.looksmart.fr
INDEXA	www.indexa.fr
KartOO	www.kartoo.com

Germany

Fireball	www.fireball.de
WEB.DE	http://web.de/?id=v00-010622-*1dap-00
AltaVista Germany	http://de.altavista.com
Lycos Germany	www.lycos.de
msn.de	http://search.msn.de
Yahoo! Deutschland	http://de.yahoo.com
Abacho	www.abacho.de
allesklar.de	www.allesklar.de
DINO-Online	www.dino-online.de
Infoseek.de	www.infoseek.de
Google Deutsch	www.google.de

UK and Germany dominate Europe in terms of internet access, with UK, Germany, Italy, and France together accounting for two-thirds of European households that are wired with internet access. Germany reported the greatest increase in the number of households with internet access in the first quarter of 2001 (Nielsen/NetRatings).

Far East

DragonField	www.dragonfield.com
goo	www.goo.ne.jp
OCN	www.ocn.ne.jp
Excite Japan	www.excite.co.jp
Google Japan	www.google.co.jp
Lycos Japan	www.lycos.co.jp
MSN Japan	http://search.msn.co.jp
Yahoo! Japan	www.yahoo.co.jp

One-third of the households in the Asia-Pacific area have internet access via home PCs. But if you want to reach Japanese consumers, you'll want to make your site wireless friendly. In Japan, people spend a lot of time commuting on trains from which they like to access the web and read email on wireless devices. You'll want to ensure your content is amenable to parsing so the new web services that parse web content for mobile phone users can extract vital data, convert it to WML (wireless markup language) and send it to all those commuters and others.

Mexico

Mexico Web	www.mexico.web.com
Mexicochannel.net	www.mexicochannel.net
inter.net	www.internet.com.mx
YupiMSN	www.yupimsn.com
MEXMASTER	www.mexmaster.com
MexSearch	www.yellow.com.mx

Statistics state that nearly half of today's on-line users are English-speaking. Global Reach estimates 147 million people from non-English-speaking countries are online now in April, 2000 (www.glreach.com/globstats), and this group will grow to 200 million by 2001 and 430 million by 2003. But according to Nicholas Negroponte (Director of the MIT Media Lab), 2002 will see towards one billion users online, because many people will be using one computer (without owning it), in third-world countries.

Spain

Yahoo! Spain	http://dir.yahoo.com/regional/countries/spain
Terra	www.terra.es
elindice	www.elindice.com
TUSPAIN	http://tuspain.com/sites/web.htm
UGABULA	http://ugabula.com

Puerto Rico

WEPA!	www.wepa.com

Brazil

Busca	http://busca.starmedia.com/strm
Cade?	www.cade.com.br
AONDE	www.aonde.com
VIA NET.WORKS	www.vianetworks.com.br/default-ie.asp
brujula.net	www.labrujula.com.ar/brazil
ondeir.com.br	www.ondier.com.br

Intelliquest research found 84 million people, in the US alone, over the age of 16 are regular internet users. Worldwide over 171 million use the web. By 2005 the total number of users is forecasted to be one BILLION people, over half of them living outside the US.

China

Yahoo! China	http://chinese.yahoo.com
SINA.com	www.sina.com
Chinese Databases	www.internets.com/schina.htm
ChinaBIG	www.chinabig.com/en/srch

Greater China Web	http://gcw.hkstar.com
Nihao Directory	www.nihao.net.ch
Chinascape	www.chinascape.org
Excite China	http://Chinese.excite.com

Taiwan

| Yam.com | www.yam.com |
| Taiwan Infoseek | www.infoseek.com.tw/index.htm |

European Search Engines, Directories and Lists

www.netmasters.co.uk/european_search_engines

Resource maintained by industry enthusiasts. It claims to be the leading directory of European search engines and directories on the internet; it is updated regularly and lists search resources that allow free registration.

International website design

Tips for designing an effective web site for global B2B:

Make it easy to pick a language
When you are dealing in a multilingual environment, one of the most important features your site can offer is clear and simple choice of language upfront. This should be among the most prominent features of a multilingual site, and it should not be tied just to the user's location or nationality because many languages cross borders. Its a good idea, experts note, to provide language choice links on each page in case the user did not start at the home page.

Route ad hoc queries
Responding to off-the-cuff inquiries is a challenge in global B2B. This is especially true in high-tech or complex purchasing decisions. An overseas engineer trying to specify a part, for example, might need quick technical support via phone from the supplier. Often, the best way to handle this is by routing such inquiries to a local partner, supplemented by an online FAQs feature.

Be concise and simplify
The more elaborate your message, and the more fancy graphics you add, the more likely you are to either confuse

your foreign audience, or turn them off. And greater complexity of content and features only adds to translation and updating costs. Also, if you start out relatively simply, there is more room for future expansion on your site.

Localise the popular cues   Much of our communication, in the business as well as the social world, relies on visual icons and slang expressions that defy simple machine or cursory human translation. It's important to check and double-check your site for symbols and cues that have entirely different meanings in foreign cultures, such as certain hand symbols, colours or catchy phrases.

Validate locally   Above all, seek local review and validation of your overseas site. While all good web designers recommend user testing, this is especially critical in the international market because of its greater diversity. Use local offices, partners or outside consultants to test and validate, and remember that usability is an issue that bears revisiting periodically.

Anticipate changing content   This affects long-range strategy for the site, including how flexible translation and updating solutions need to be, and what the trade-offs may be between the geographical reach of the site or its level of sophistication for a particular audience. For companies that anticipate continuously changing content, it's often prudent to select an outside globalization/translation expert to assist with site development.

Limit user options   Many current sites allow the user many options by letting them 'fill in the blank,' as in 'my alternate preference would be – ' In the case of multilingual sites, however, this is not usually a good idea because it complicates translation because of differences in linguistic structures. For example, adjectives precede nouns in English, but not in many other languages such as French and Spanish.

Where to look for information

Transparent Language Inc – www.freetranslation.com
This site showcases the company's product, Enterprise Translation Server,

which can be integrated into a company's internet or communications applications as an add-on module. The product can also be tailored to a specific industry e.g. computer, hotel and tourism, increasing the likelihood of correct translations for more complex words and phrases. Additionally, you can link your web site to FreeTranslation.com, allowing your site visitors who speak French, German, Italian, Spanish and Portuguese to view your site in their native languages.

Smart Link Corporation – www.paralink.com/translation
This site sponsors a site that has similar capabilities to FreeTranslation's, though it also includes Russian.

Lernout & Hauspie's Power Translator – www.lhsl.com/powertranslator
This family of products has been integrated with Microsoft Office 2000 to help preserve document formatting.

Where can you go to get a comprehensive picture of a country's buying population?

- **Consultants.** Andersen Consulting and other global consultancies can provide some information. Analyst firms IDC, Gartner, Forrester, Jupiter, and others have each created a global opportunity index, but each firm offers different recommendations due to their differing methodologies. For example, IDC and Gartner concentrate on installed devices and Internet infrastructure, while Jupiter and Forrester rely on infrequently updated indices of variables.
- **Informational sites.** A few web sites provide varying degrees of detail about different markets. Portals at vendor and globalization providers can be helpful, such as **www.idiominc.com/worldwise**, as are sites specializing in statistical overviews, such as **www.nua.ie** or **www.cyberatlas.com** and **www.e-marketer.com**.

The good news is that most of the companies that assemble components and manufacture products are used to producing items to a number of different specifications in order to meet the requirements of each country. If you wish to get an insight into how this works, visit Global Sources (**www.v2gsol. globalsources.com/gsol/owa/product.level/home.htm**). There you will be able to source a manufacturer for any of 82,000 products in 2,900 categories in 150 countries. A basic search of the web will also provide you with contact information for numerous consultancies that specialise in helping marketers with international product specifications.

You can find downloadable web reports to purchase titled 'Global Internet Markets – Statistics Overviews' at Paul Budde Communication (**www.budde.com.au**). The reports provide regional, country, and language updates. ACNielsen (**www.eratings.com**) offers information on global measurement of Internet penetration for 17 countries across Europe and Asia-Pacific. A key point here is that the data was collected on a consistent basis and should therefore be comparable.

A site that provide free data about internet penetration by country is Nua (**www.nua.com**). Although this is a compilation of information from different sources and with different dates -- and therefore not all of the data is strictly comparable – it provides good insight into the development of the web around the world.

Four secrets for those just entering the global B2B marketplace

1 – Globalization equals professionalisation

One of the most important things to do early on is to conduct an assessment of readiness and to formulate a strategy. Consultants and analysts like IDC's (**www.idc.com**) Anna Giraldo-Kerr question the wisdom of moving too quickly, before readiness to globalize is established. 'Once you have a web site, you have a global presence. You have to be ready to respond professionally to potential foreign opportunities,' she says. 'Companies that want to globalize need to look first at issues of demand – where are the potential business partners who want to trade with me, or whom I want to buy from? Then, you need to think about the technical hurdles, like who's online, how good the telecomm net-work is in that country or region. Is this market equipped to handle widespread web communication?'

2 – Learn the art of multicultural deal-making

Often, global marketers falsely assume that the only significant barrier between them and their overseas counterparts is language. Not so, analysts and experts say. In fact, differences in culture may be the most important factor to consider in global B2B.

Many globalization consultants note that web sites aimed at overseas partners must be localised, not only linguistically, but in terms of presentation and content. It's important to validate your site vis-à-vis the local culture to avoid gaffes like using green in some Muslim countries where it is considered sacred. Another aspect of doing deals abroad relates to differences in what is an accept-able way to conduct transactions.

3 – Pay attention to content management

The global challenge of today's increasingly dynamic content will only become more complicated, according to those knowledgeable about the globalization business. Early global web sites, whether by design or by accident, were often predicated on a more static model. This pre-supposed a turnaround time that would allow content to be evaluated for relevance, then translated, then routed. The challenge now, the experts say, is to process a high volume of multilingual data or content all the time, coming from everywhere.

4 – Leverage local relationships

The multicultural nature of global business creates a degree of complexity that can't be easily satisfied just by establishing a web presence, the experts say. Businesses cannot underestimate the value of a local presence and the insight that having an on-site window into the culture represents. Local partners can help provide the answer to problems of trade regulation and tariffs, and legal and regulatory complexities.

10

Forming Strategic Partnerships
and Links

CLICK-ONS

Strategic partnerships

Making links

Portal links

Strategic partnerships

Strategic Partnerships is the new marketing buzzword on the internet. Strategic partnerships are arrangements between two websites, where one website provides a service or information to visitors of the other website in exchange for visitors. A link encouraging visitors to visit the website or names and email addresses for an email marketing campaign are the most common ways to exchange visitors. Strategic partnerships have proven particularly effective with portal websites that get phenomenal amounts of traffic, like Yahoo. If your website offers a valuable service, especially if it uses a cgi program nobody else seems to have, consider talking to the big websites about letting them access your service in return for prominent credit and a link to your website. For the rest of us, strategic partnerships will be much more low-key, but still effective. Find websites, which offer services, related to your own which are not direct competitors. Think of something you can offer their visitors that they can't, and offer it to them in exchange for a link. If your website doesn't offer a service or valuable information others would want to offer on their website, consider joint advertising ventures or contests.

If you want more customers, consider trading your Thank You space for space on a related website with a similar target audience. Thank you space is one of the best places to advertise, because people who have just completed a transaction are in the mood to make another. Plus, they are ready to move on to another website, having finished their business on the website where you're advertising. Also consider approaching a company with the same target market directly. If they want your customers, they may be willing to pay you for the traffic they get from your website, how many people complete the form you offer, etc.

Making links

Some websites, usually directories, ask you to pay for listings or listing upgrades. Upgrading your listing makes it more visible, usually putting it at or near the top of the list. Unless the directory is popular and specialises in your industry or locality, don't do it. Even if the directory is popular, consider their offer carefully, comparing it to other advertising methods. Spend your energy on the more popular search engines instead. Pay-for-listing directories will not likely bring you an amount of traffic worth the investment.

Ask other business owners who work with similar clients to send an endorsed mailing to their clients on your behalf. To work best, they should have experienced the value of your products or services for themselves and really believe in them. Then give them a special offer or free gift (such as a special report) of extraordinary value that they can offer their clients. They will receive goodwill for sending the extraordinary offer, and you will receive a credible testimonial for your product and a substantial number of new leads!

Free For All links pages list any websites willing to submit to them by category. Often they delete their oldest links after they have a certain number of submissions, so their pages don't get too long. These link pages are not searchable, so keywords aren't as important. Sometimes, they don't even offer a description of the pages in their list. Instead, they always put the most recently submitted website at the top of the list. Free For All Links pages are not a very popular way to find websites, and your listing may be squeezed off the list within a few days, if not hours. Basically, they are created to boost traffic for the website hosting them by attracting people with websites they want to promote. You might be able to increase your traffic by submitting to popular Free For All Links pages. If you really want to try Free For All Links, go for a service or program that will submit your website and description to hundreds of link pages in a few minutes, then submit all the pages you submitted to search engines. Re-submit your website to this type of webpage at least once a week. If nothing else, major search engines will notice more sites linking to yours, and some might boost your rankings because of it (like HotBot).

When visitors see a link on their favourite website, they tend to believe it is there because the company or webmaster liked that website more than all its competitors. They are more likely to visit it, and more likely to buy from it, than a visitor who found your website in another way.

Are you asking websites with content related to yours to link to your website? Non-commercial links pages have an authority all other methods (other than testimonials) lack. Not to mention that they improve your search engine rankings. When asking for links from other websites, always give the webmaster benefits of linking to your website (both to their visitors and to them). Offering to link back to their website is not only polite, it also increases the likelihood of their taking you up on the offer. Links on other websites can increase your traffic in two ways: by giving potential visitors a way to find your website, and by increasing your ranking in search engines which use link popularity as part of their formula. Listings on popular websites can be a more significant source of traffic than search engines for some websites! The wonderful thing about links pages is the credibility they offer your website. Each link is like having a testimonial for your website on somebody else's website.

There are two barriers to getting listed on other peoples' websites. You have to find websites where visitors will be interested in the content of your website, and you have to convince the webmaster or website owner to link to your website.

Because this is a very personal process, you can't rely on an outside service to solicit links for your website. You must approach each website individually and tailor your message to them. Since any attempt to get links through mass mailings will fail, soliciting links can be very time consuming. This process can be automated by gathering a list of websites with content related to yours with a program like Web Ferret (**www.ferretsoft.com/netferret/download.htm**). You can also find email addresses on those websites and automatically send them a message, using a template email customised a little for each website with 2bpop. **www.2bpop.com**.

Search for sites which attract the sort of visitors you want at your site. Preferably, the content of your target website will be related to your own. For example, if you sell shoes, get a link on walking and hiking websites. Being linked on related websites will boost your search engine rankings a little extra. Next, make sure the websites you have targeted have links to other websites, preferably websites similar to your own. Does that hiking website already link to Water Bottles R Us? If so, your shoe store has a good chance. If they just link to National Parks and Local Hiking Trails, emailing them could be a waste of time. TIP: You might want to ask for banner rates if they don't list websites like yours.

> Finding well-designed, popular websites with content, which attracts your website's intended audience, isn't easy, but it is the key to successful link solicitation campaigns. You can ask for and receive links from anyone, but none of them will drive traffic to your website like a good one with related content.

So, you have some websites worthy of a link to your website. How do you get them to list it with keywords in the anchor (the blue underlined bit) to boost your search engine rankings as much as possible? Sometimes, just telling a website that you are on the web and giving them a short keyword-laden description is enough. If they know and like you or your company, it probably will be that easy. Here are some tips:

- Tell the webmaster or website owner the benefits a link to your website will offer their visitors.
- Offer the webmaster or website owner a benefit of linking to your website: a reciprocal link, an ad or endorsement in your ezine, money for referring buyers, or even a free gift.

- Write your email in plain text. Even if you have an email program, which will allow you to use HTML formatting, resist the urge. It takes longer to load, and often annoys people, especially if their email program doesn't support it.
- Write your email message offline. It will give you a chance to mull it over without pressure and with a spell-checker. Always include your website address, complete with 'http://' so it will show up as a link in their email and print out if they save it for later.
- Use a title for your website which uses keywords that will attract visitors without a separate description. If it starts with a letter at the beginning of the alphabet, even better.

If you have links from other web pages, but they don't seem to be bringing you any traffic after a few weeks, visit the links pages. Are your links visible? Are other people visiting the page? Try to find the links page from the websites' home pages. If it's difficult, you have your answer. Otherwise, the website(s) you are listed on may not be popular enough, or you may be approaching the wrong target audience. Don't waste your time on websites with unrelated content or those who focus on a different type of visitor. Spend that extra time developing an email message which will sell your website to people capable of driving traffic to you, and who you would be proud to link to on your website.

Do not link to your homepage in your ads. If a potential customer gets interested in a new product or service, you should not force him to find out how to navigate the site from the homepage to the relevant page. Instead, link directly to the relevant page from the ad. Also, seed press releases with specific URLs that support your message: reporters may follow these links for additional detail and online publications may use specific links instead of generic ones to better serve their users. If you are running a campaign with a certain theme, have it include a URL to a page that follows up on that theme. The payoff page should not be a copy of the ad (the customer presumably already read the ad before going to the web), though a link to an online version of the ad might be appropriate to help users who go to the page without having seen the ad. Instead, use each medium for what it's good at. For example, a training company could use trade magazine advertising to make people think that a particular course looks good and use the web to allow them to interact with a simplified version of the course.

How do you get others to link to your site? Here are some ideas:

- You could offer an award that other quality internet marketing sites are eligible to win. As the award is displayed on winning sites, it will bring traffic to your site.
- You probably belong to various trade associations that feature member sites. Ask for a link. Even if you have to pay something for a link, it may bring you the kind of targeted traffic you need.
- You would give away valuable prizes every month. All the entrants have to do in order to be eligible is to link up with your site.
- You would allow others to make money by selling your products via a secure ordering page for all associates. All they have to do is link to it from their site.
- Find complementary websites and request a reciprocal link to your site (especially to your free service, if you offer one). Develop an out-of-the way page where you put links to other sites.
- Request links from business link sites. Especially if you offer a free service, you can request links from many of the small business linking pages on the web. Surf the net looking for places that might link to your site. Then email the site owner or webmaster with your site name, URL, and a brief 200-word description of what you offer there.

Portal links

Can you say with 100 percent certainty that you have maximized your links across the major portals? As the search engines and directories partner up with each other, with paid link providers, with reviewers, with product databases, with news providers, with advertisers, with anyone they think can help them build a better service, the result from a linking perspective is a bevy of new linking opportunities that didn't exist a year ago.

Take a site like Google. A link to your site can come from Google in at least three ways, some paid, some free. Google pulls links from three different sets of data. Google takes the words you are searching for and passes them through four different databases on the way to presenting the results to you. The first database is Google's own index (**www.google.com/addurl.html**) of millions of web pages. The second database is Netscape's Open Directory (**http://directory.google.com**). The third database is the paid AdWords program database (**https://adwords.google.com/adwords/welcome.html**), and the last database is the paid banner advertising (**www.goggle.com/ads/index.html**) database. So, there are four ways your link could appear to a Google searcher. You have to decide which of those four databases you want to be in and whether it's free or costs you a little money to do so. At Yahoo!, there are as many as seven different sets of data from which a link to your site could come. There's the basic Yahoo! category listing, but have you checked into the six others? And at AOL, a searcher could find your links in at least four different databases. The key is two-sided:

- make sure you understand which databases are being queried for each search
- determine what it takes to be in as many of those databases as possible.

Conduct a portal link audit for your site and maybe even for your competitors. Find those places where you could be linked. You can be sure your competitor is doing it. Many sites could double or triple the number of links they have with little expense and a little time. Every new portal partnership could mean a new way your link could make it to the results page.

Making links

- **AOL invests $100 million in Amazon.com:** America Online will make a $100 million equity investment in e-commerce giant Amazon.com as the two companies launch a multi-year alliance in which they will build up America Online's interactive brands and beef up its online retail presence. The companies will work on e-commerce initiatives like customer authentication and wallet services and they will combine Amazon.com's technology with AOL's online presence to strengthen Shop@AOL. Amazon.com will also make AOL its exclusive internet service provider, enabling its customers to download the AOL service from different areas with in its site. Amazon.com will promote AOL Time-Warner products, as well.

- **Nestlé promoting pet products with AOL**: Nestlé USA has tapped America Online to help promote Friskies Petcare products online. Under the agreement, Friskies will be featured in the 'House and Home' channels of the AOL and CompuServe services and will also be promoted on AOL's Digital City. These promotions will offer links to the Friskies.com site. While AOL is one of the web's most popular marketing partners, the alliance makes even more sense considering AOL's assertion that nearly 70 percent of its members own pets.

- **Sony and Yahoo! in marketing deal:** Sony Corp. of America will be advertising with web portal Yahoo!, in a multi-year deal that sees Yahoo! following America Online's lead in striking partnerships with consumer electronics leaders. Through the deal, Yahoo! will create a co-branded content area, dubbed 'Sony on My Yahoo!'. The site will incorporate personalised content from Yahoo!'s My Yahoo page, but will be geared for Sony enthusiasts, with links to the company's products and news. In conjunction with Sony on My Yahoo!, the Sunnyvale, California-based portal also said it would create co-branded versions of the Yahoo! Companion Web browser toolbar and Yahoo! Messenger instant message application.

  The Sony on My Yahoo! effort comes in addition to more direct pitches to Yahoo!'s audiences for the consumer products colossus' wares. For instance, New York-based Sony's SonyStyle.com e-commerce site will receive prominent placement on Yahoo! Shopping, and throughout the Yahoo! site. Ads for specific Sony products also will run throughout Yahoo! Sony also said it would use the portal to promote movie releases from its Sony Pictures Entertainment division. Specifically, Sony said it would run online ad promotions for its upcoming films 'Ali,' 'The Panic Room' and 'Deeds.' In return for all of this marketing consideration, Yahoo! stands to benefits from increased exposure to Sony customers, which tend toward the higher end among buyers of consumer electronics. For one, Sony's VAIO computers will be preloaded with software to register for membership on Yahoo! and for product information from Sony. Additionally, Sony on My Yahoo! also will become the default start page of Sony's ISP service, Sony Style Connect. Finally, Yahoo! also will take home a consulting contract for a revamp of Sony's US corporate portal, which the firms said they envision becoming an 'interconnected web community' of Sony product users.

- **Amazon.com teams with AT&T Wireless:** Online retailer Amazon.com has teamed with AT&T Wireless to give AT&T Digital PocketNet customers access to the Amazon.com wireless web site on their internet-ready wireless phones. Using the Amazon Anywhere platform, wireless customers can access Amazon.com for purchasing, getting product recommendations, customer reviews and search features. 'By accessing virtually all of our catalogue via their mobile devices, AT&T Wireless' mobile Internet customers will be able to shop with Amazon.com more conveniently and with greater ease than ever before,' said Robert Frederick, Manager, Amazon Anywhere. 'Over the past two years, we have been hard at work developing the best mobile commerce platform tailored to meet our customers' changing needs.'

- **AOL, Universal expand alliance:** America Online and Universal Pictures have extended the two companies' marketing alliance to include promotion of the studio's products across AOL Time Warner's combination of on-air and online media properties. Under the new agreement, several of Universal Pictures' new releases will receive wide promotion across a variety of AOL Time Warner media, including television networks such as The WB and Turner Broadcasting's TNT; America Online brands such as AOL, AOL Moviefone and AOL By Phone; and additional AOL Time Warner online properties, such as ENTERTAINMENTWEEKLY.com, PEOPLE.com and TheWB.com.

- **AOL adds Samsung to ads roster:** AOL Time Warner and Samsung Electronics are joining for a new strategic marketing and technology development alliance. Under the terms of the multi-year agreement, AOL TW will help promote the Samsung brand through its various media channels, including 'People,' 'Entertainment Weekly' and 'Sports Illustrated' magazines, the AOL service and Moviefone.com. AOL TW will also promote Samsung's forthcoming PDA mobile phone in an integrated marketing campaign. Other programs include a promotion of Samsung's HDTV across print, online and TV, and a 'Countdown to the Olympics' contest in which AOL members can register to win Samsung prizes, as well as learn more about the winter games in the months leading up to the 2002 Winter Olympics. Samsung and AOL TW will also collaborate on the development and marketing of a next generation AOLTV set top box that includes recording capability via the TiVo service.

- **Yahoo!, British bank ally on online payment:** Yahoo! and British banking and financial services group HSBC Holdings say they want to bring online payments out of the dark ages. The two companies have made a deal to launch a co-branded, person-to-person payment system called Yahoo! PayDirect with HSBC. The service would be available to Yahoo! and HSBC customers and is expected to launch later this year. The new online payment service will let consumers send and receive money, at home and overseas, via e-mail by linking their credit cards, debit cards or bank accounts to their Yahoo! PayDirect account at HSBC. The companies say the platform can also be used to electronically send money as a gift to family and friends, to collect contributions to group or charity events, and to pay for shopping and auctions purchases. Yahoo! already has established its http://banking.yahoo.com/ >Yahoo! Banking and Yahoo! Bill Pay for people who want to pay utilities and other online financial transactions, but this marks the first time by Yahoo! to establish a person-to-person payment plan. Because financial transactions are subject to certain regulatory approvals, Yahoo! PayDirect with HSBC will launch first in the US. After that and throughout 2002, the service will be extended to other countries and areas where HSBC and Yahoo! operate. Santa Clara, California-based Yahoo! and London-based HSBC say the goal is to make the Yahoo! PayDirect technology available to other companies to enable commerce and person-to-person payment capabilities.

'With this agreement, HSBC becomes our global financial partner, helping ready us for our next phase of growth and further extending our financial and commerce services,' says Yahoo! executive VP Greg Coleman. HSBC says it will also mount a comprehensive online and offline marketing program to make their products and services available to Yahoo!'s 200 million consumers. Yahoo! in turn will similarly market its services to HSBC's 28 million customers.

- **NASA tests internet marketing to gather thousands of qualified business partnership leads:** As Director of Marketing for NASA Commercial Technology Programs, it's Michael Weingarten's job to funnel NASA's tech discoveries to American industry by locating the right point person in each company that might be interested in developing a new product based on NASA's inventions.

Back when he started this project seven years ago, he invented a lead generation program from scratch. Weingarten set up a toll-free phone number for inquiries, created a customer service centre to handle them, and rolled out direct mail and print ad campaigns to drive callers. But about a year ago, he began to wonder if the whole process could be handled more efficiently on the internet. Like many large, decentralised organisations, NASA's biggest challenge in transitioning to web marketing wasn't the web itself. Instead, the initial challenge was an internal one. Almost 40 marketers are responsible for various NASA programs at 10 different research centres across the country. This decentralised system meant that Weingarten had to not only get detailed product information from each and every marketer, he also had to get everyone to buy-in to the idea of a centralised web marketing program. This took about a year. Then with the help of B2B agency Kern Direct, Weingarten created a web site to capture partnership leads, as well as a system to process those leads quickly and to efficiently funnel the hottest ones to just the right NASA contact for their particular needs. The site, NASATechnology.com, captures leads in three different ways:

1. **Free offer**: The home page features a prominent offer for 'Spin Off Magazine', a glossy four-colour magazine that highlights the stories of how 30 different companies in a wide range of industries partnered with NASA to create new products. When prospects click on the free magazine offer, they see a pop-up box requesting their snail mail address.

2. **Enticing navigation**: The site's home page also features a left-side navigation bar listing 12 different types of technology alphabetically, from aerodynamics to telecommunications. When visitors click on any of those links to explore a particular section, a brief form appears saying, 'Before proceeding, we need to find out a little bit about you. Please note that there is no charge to register for this service.' The only information requested is name, company, city, state and email. (The system automatically captures which topical link the visitor clicked on and feeds this information into the database as well.)

3. **Search requests**: Every time a visitor use the search box for a particular term, a bright button that says, 'I'm interested!' pops up next to the search results. Visitors who click on this button are immediately directed through the CRM system so a customer service person can take the next step either by phone or email.

As the site captures leads, they are fed through to Weingarten's customer service centre and assigned a priority action code. The hottest leads are culled so a trained rep can immediately begin the process of qualifying them, and then getting them in touch with the appropriate person in NASA's far-flung organisation. From that point, the cycle for closing deals can take up to another year because often millions are at stake. Weingarten tested marketing campaigns in three different media to drive qualified traffic to the site – space ads in magazines, direct postal mail to rented lists and direct email to rented opt-in lists.

He chose highly targeted media, such as 'Chemical Engineering' as well as testing broader interest publications such as 'Fast Company. NASA has gathered more than a thousand hot, qualified leads for its industry partner program since the NASATechnology.com site launched in February 2001, while achieving significant cost savings per lead. Sales leads include members of the Fortune 500, as well as many mid-sized companies.

Weingarten has found that email marketing is more cost-effective than print ads or direct postal mail. While running campaigns with identical offers to all three media, often to the same lists (a magazine, its snail mail list and its email list), Weingarten got response rates of .5% for print ads, 2% for direct mail and around 9% for email. The lists that worked best were very niche. On the site itself, the navigation bar options were twice as effective at gathering leads than the colourful free offer was! This is dramatic news for other B2B marketers relying on a free offer alone at a web-landing page to gather sales leads.

11

Tracking and Evaluating Your Marketing Response

CLICK-ONS

Analysing traffic

Measuring results

Using data analysis to increase buying

Analysing traffic

Your hard work and persistence in optimising your pages have resulted in a dramatic increase in traffic to your site, which is just what you wanted. But, are you analysing that traffic and using it to strengthen your site? Or, are you quickly glancing at your log files every week or so to see how much traffic you're getting, and letting it go at that? What exactly are log files? When someone visits your web site, server software counts and tracks or logs that visit. It also keeps a record of it for a certain period of time. Part of the saved information is called a referrer log. Referrer logs can help you analyse the traffic to your site. By default, a log file for a site is stored in the root directory, and is compiled automatically as visitors pass through a site. Where would you find your log file? If your web site is www.overtheweb.com, the log file would be in the directory that held your default.html (or index.html or home.html, depending on what you called it) file. If you're working with a reputable web presence provider, there may be some reports available to you. WebTrends (**www.webtrends.com**) is probably the most popular software available to use. It creates impressive and useful reports. Though each referrer log program provides slightly different data, some of the more common information includes:

- average length of time someone remains on your site
- how many people have visited your site
- which page they left the site from – if certain pages always seem to cause people to leave your site then those are candidates to be enhanced to encourage people to stay longer and buy something
- average number of user sessions or page views per day
- top entry and exit pages
- top referring sites
- summary of activity by day
- server errors
- how many pages each person viewed
- the average time people spent on each page
- the number of users for particular day, week or month and usage by time of day
- which companies are using your site
- the home city or country that users are coming from
- which pages were accessed the most or the least
- who are the visiting spiders
- user profile by region
- what the first page of your web site viewed by each user – this is important if you want to get an idea how people are finding your site
- bandwidth, which is the measure (in kilobytes of data transferred) of the traffic on the site
- type of technology used by your visitors
- number of successful participants (how well the list worked)
- referral sites (where leads/visitors come from)
- placement on search engines and specific target referral sites
- performance of affiliate sites (if included in the program)
- number of click-throughs (visitors who moved deeper into the content)
- ratio of visitors to customers (buyers)
- most and least successful content (visitors and time spent)
- most and least popular products/content
- feedback

- unsubscribes (people who leave your list or community because the value isn't there)
- customer satisfaction (if you give them the option to vote)
- which engines have sent you traffic
- what keywords were used to find your site.

Hacker alert

There may be types of data that you can't find in a log file or that your web server isn't collecting. If that's the case for you, see if your web server can log more data than you're currently collecting, or if there are COM objects or plug-ins available for your server that would allow you to collect more data. Close analysis of your web traffic can help you determine whether a competitor is spidering your site either to check your prices or to steal your content.

Through your referrer logs, you'll probably discover that you're getting found through keyword phrases that you haven't even considered before. In that case, you certainly don't want to change those pages and lose the traffic. By the same token, if you're getting found under a keyword phrase in one engine, wouldn't it be worth creating pages for the other engines for that same keyword phrase to see if you can bring in some additional traffic? Simply put, a referrer log can give you an enormous amount of information and can serve as a road map for future changes to your site.

Hits are the old way to measure site popularity. Every time your page is loaded, your server counts it as a hit. The problem with this measure is that it's estimated that as much as 1/3 of all site traffic is by spiders, which are programs that crawl the web, either as part of a search engine or looking for e-mail addresses. This means that as much as 1/3 of all requests for your home page are never seen by human eyes. A more meaningful statistic to you is the number of unique visitors. By collecting the IP address of visitors, or by placing cookies on the browsers of visitors, you can determine how many actual visitors have seen your site.

Once you are getting some business through your web site and you are relatively happy with the amount of traffic or hits on your web site, it is important to do some analysis of the usage and make adjustments to your web site to maximise the business. Even the smallest ISPs generally allows access to an access log which records traffic to a web site. These logs record an entry for every page (or graphic) requested from your site and usually has some sort of identifier (such as IP address) of the person requesting the page. Some ISPs offer their own analysis tools or scripts to view this activity but if not, there are several tools available which produce detailed reports and graphs of activity on your site. If you use Microsoft's Site Manager V3.0 to develop and manage your site, it already includes a number of custom analysis reports as well as the ability to create new ones.

WebAlyser lets you build a database of your access log reports and create reports and graphs using any combination of the following information:

- The date, day and/or hour a visitor came.

- The length of the visit.

- The browser type and version.

- The operating system used by the visitor (You will have to tell the program which visitors are using newer operating systems, like Windows 98, 2000 and XP. It takes a long time, but will be worth it if the information is vital to your website's functionality or your products.)

- The bandwidth used.

- Places people visited on your website (Usually directories, but you can customise it).

You can uncover information most website analysis programs never touch such as:

- Are my visitors staying longer on certain days of the week?

- Are people using a certain browser or operating system leaving my website, indicating a problem?

- Which pages are visitors going to? Which are they avoiding?

- If visitors are coming in to my website in this directory, which directory do they visit next?

Don't expect charts of how many hits you got on which day or lists of websites sending you traffic. There will be no list of the phrases people are using to find your website in search engines, either. This information is vital, but you'll have to find it elsewhere. Use WebAlyser in addition to your host's statistics, a good counter, or another website log analysis program. Download the free 30-day trial today at **www.webalyser.com**.

Other traffic issues worth analysing:

- What browsers are most frequently used by your visitors? Check this section periodically to make sure that the technology offered at your web site can be used by the majority of your visitors. In other words, if many of your visitors are accessing the web using older browsers, you will want to be careful about using technology that will prevent them from fully utilising your web site.
- What are the top referring sites and URLs?
- What are the top referring search engines? Do you have some top ranking pages in certain search engines, but you're not seeing coinciding traffic through those engines? If so, you may need to rethink your keyword strategy.
- Which search engine spiders have visited your site recently? After submitting your pages to the engines, be sure to monitor this section closely for spider activity. Keep track of when a spider hits your site and how deep and compare it to the dates you submit and the dates the pages actually appear in the index. You will start to see a pattern emerge with each engine.
- If you want a corner of the international market, study this data carefully. How many user sessions are being generated for each country that's important to your business? How you can beef up efforts to improve those numbers? Are you creating highly targeted information pages for your international keywords?
- What are the keywords that searchers are using to find your site? If you're being found under a particular keyword in one engine but not another, boost efforts in the other search engine and try to bring in more traffic. Also, study this section closely for any holes in your keyword-thinking strategies. Remember that search engine positioning strategies begin with a simple keyword or keyword phrase. If you're having problems finding a keyword phrase that will bring you more traffic, visit WordTracker (**www.wordtracker.com**) and sign up for their free trial service, Or visit GoTo's Search Term Suggestion List (**http://inventory. goto.com/d/searchinventory/suggestion**). Also, most search engines have 'related search' results that can give you some clues, so don't over look that information.

- Which pages are being viewed by themselves, where visitors aren't even clicking to go to another page? You're losing them, and you need to figure out why.
- If your visitors encounter too many error messages, e.g. 404 pages, when visiting your web site, they'll assume that you don't do your 'house cleaning,' and the professional image of your site will plummet.

> When you are stumped as to why none of the words you optimised for are hitting, look at the logs. Use the words you see actually hitting with the search engines in your reporting files (WebPosition Gold). It can help you find more avenues of traffic. At the very least, you can show some positions because you are showing some traffic from the engines.

Measuring results

Why is it so important to study your traffic? Isn't it enough to know that your traffic is increasing, without having to spend valuable time analysing it? If you know which engines are sending you the most traffic, you can boost your optimisation strategies for those engines by creating additional pages for other relevant keyword phrases. This could increase your traffic even more. Or, if you know that you're not getting any traffic at all from a particular engine, you'll be able to consider strategies for findability on that engine.

> The time users spend at a site tells me if they are actually reading the site or just clicking in only to leave immediately. Perhaps I am not conveying the purpose of the site well enough to make them stay. Or, I am listed under the wrong phrases. If I am buying traffic from GoTo or another engine, I like to know if the words I chose are valuable to me or just a waste. Which page is attracting the most visits and how long are they there? This helps me decide what areas of a site need to be expanded upon and what areas can be dropped. For an example with a sports picks site, we found that the least visited page was the record the handicapper used to show everyone his win/lose ratio for picks and the chat room. So we dropped the page and spent the programming money on live scores and a sports news page.
>
> Ginette Degner, professional optimiser with
> SearchEngineServices.com

You should also look at: Top entry pages and how are people first coming in to your site? Which pages are bringing you the most traffic? What about some of your other pages? What can you do to make them top entry pages too? Exit pages are another very important area of a log file, according to Degner:

? Where are they leaving?
? What off site links are they clicking on the most?
? If this is an intro page or another sub page that is a doorway, I may need to get rid of it or use a redirect
? It tells me where I am losing visitors.

Using data analysis to increase buying

How do we use data analytics to determine which customers are worth encouraging? Use your tracking capabilities to follow that shopping cart around and watch for the behaviours that distinguish the surfers and browsers from those who complete a transaction. Then track those distinctions back to the source of the initial lead to look for patterns. Though many marketers source a successful transaction back to the site it linked in from, few take the necessary next step to source the creative message that generated the link. Those who do often find that appropriately targeted messaging have a lot to do with which new arrivals become customers.

Perhaps the more important application for analytics here, however, is a focus on increasing purchase likelihood rather than just on understanding those who purchase. Smart retailers look for displays that cause shoppers to lose interest; online sellers should do the same. When you see a correlation between cart abandonment and a particular point in your site, experiment with changes to the site before assuming that the customer is necessarily the problem. If you set up your web analytics to track behaviour, you'll optimise that effort by also setting up your site to easily enable revision, and then you'll test for changes in results. Profitability comes from knowing who to focus your marketing message on, learning how to improve the buying experience of those you do attract, and increasing their propensity to complete the sale as well as to increase the size or frequency of sales.

Customer life cycle

In the model of a customer life cycle, the marketer pays attention to these key steps along the buying continuum:

1	**Reach:**	Claim someone's attention.
2	**Acquisition:**	Bring that person into your sphere of influence.
3	**Conversion:**	Turn that person into a paying customer.
4	**Retention:**	Keep that person as a customer.
5	**Loyalty:**	Turn that person into a company advocate.

Ideally, a prospect is led through all those steps and kept satisfied enough to repeat the steps when the next purchase is called for; in reality, however, 'fallout' can occur at each step along the way. Because buyers can abandon a solution or be diverted to another one at so many points in the buying life cycle, marketers who pay close attention to behaviours at and between each step will learn just where their marketing efforts are most vulnerable to attack from competitors or, worse, inertia.

Web marketers will disagree whether reach is achieved when an ad is displayed (an impression) or when the ad is clicked. Some would call this step acquisition, but it certainly does not equal purchase. In the traditional media world, reach is accomplished when the message is seen (or presumed to be seen, in that the viewer could have seen the advert). In general, reach, online or offline, does not require proof that the advertising message was viewed, read, studied, or paid attention to, but it does assume that some attention to the message was possible, perhaps even likely. Bringing the prospect into the marketer's sphere of influence might be considered acquisition, though many of us prefer to measure acquisition only when a name or contact information is captured or the prospective buyer makes a purchase or takes some other purposeful action. The rest of the steps are pretty self-explanatory, but the evidence of turning a customer into an advocate will require some careful thought for each type of product or service, making this another rather difficult metric to generalise. Think about how customers tend to interact with your product and what the impact of word-of-mouth praise (or word-of-mouth criticism) tends to be, and you'll be able to come up with some useful measurements of this last element.

Buying processes and data analysis

Trying to make the web measurable without first understanding which measurements are most important adds enormously to the frustration, cost, and time commitment of achieving a satisfactory data-analysis solution. The raw data coming off any sizeable web site is so copious, so unmanageable, that analysis paralysis is sure to set in unless you first take the time to determine which measures, and which data, actually matter to your intended results. Awareness of need, awareness of solutions, fact finding, persuasion, transaction, postsale information, and support: those are many of the steps a buyer goes through when making a purchase decision. The importance of any one step varies depending on the product, service, category, distribution arrangement, and lots of intangibles like market conditions and brand perception.

Are you introducing a whole new category of product, never before offered? You may need to focus the bulk of your marketing effort on creating a need. The right metrics here will reflect your success at making buyers aware that they have a problem – and one you can solve. If you are selling a lower-cost 'me too' entry in a crowded commodity-like market, the early steps may be safely assumed to be covered; your marketing effort has to focus on the information-gathering and persuasion stages. If that product is a high-end offering sold by a direct sales force, marketing may be best deployed in providing information, letting the persuasion happen face to face. If you sell through multi-tier distribution, perhaps you can't rely on your channel to effectively persuade, and your marketing goals have to expand to include that piece. Either way, you won't be interested in online advertising data that deals in clicks or traffic; your focus will be on whether competitive, actionable buying information is being disseminated by your web site, and whether that information is effective enough to send buyers out to the channel to complete the transaction.

Tracking and measuring buyer behaviour

The next step in planning how to analyse customer data is to acknowledge that even within a common framework, customers are still individuals and will choose to approach the purchase process in individual and personal ways. Whereas one customer may be totally data-driven, another may make decisions intuitively. One may actively seek third-party opinions from trusted sources, while another may prefer to base decisions on personal experience. Some of us respond well to visual clues, choosing to learn from demos and comparison charts, while others respond more strongly to verbal pitches or emotional cues. The overall buying process can follow a fairly predictable format, but the individual process will always be personal. This is equally true in the B2B world. Your web site is most effective when each customer can accomplish information-gathering and decision-making goals in his or her own way, handle the transaction the way he or she would prefer, and communicate any post-sale support needs in a way that personally suits him or her.

Great web sites allow customers the option to do business the way the customer wants to, not just the one way the site expects. This makes data analysis tricky, because you won't know which behaviours to measure until you have some sense of the various ways prospects and customers choose to navigate your site. It's easy to assume that an abandoned shopping cart means the prospect was not really interested or that net security was the stopping point. But if the prospect signed off right after checking your shipping page, you may have an indication that the problem was shipping cost, or the expected time of arrival, or the knowledge that you don't use environmentally friendly packaging materials. If the departure occurs at the credit information page, there may be a security concern, or the shopper is impatient with having to retype a card number or irritated at having to sign in again when the password is not recalled. To get the most out of customer data, we need to put ourselves into the customer's mindset, think as broadly as possible about what various behaviours might mean, and then test those assumptions with real people.

> The best and most cost effective way to track your web site is you can install a CGI script onto your web site's server. You will need to have a CGI-BIN and to be able to add scripts to it. If you are not sure if you have full access to your CGI-BIN, then you need to ask your web hosting provider. There are many free CGI scripts available online that can do as many features as the top software programs that sell for 600 dollars. You can get access to over 50 CGI scripts here: **http://cgi.resourceindex.com/Programs_and_Scripts/Perl/ Logging_Accesses_and_Statistics/**

Clear marketing objectives drive good analytics

Site traffic, though a necessary data point for determining capital requirements and bandwidth constraints, is not very helpful to the marketer whose aim is larger average order size, more frequent visits from prior customers, lower incidence of product returns, or whatever other criteria have been identified as leading to increased revenue and profitability. Great marketing organisations don't focus on generic goals such as 'getting the word out'; they look several levels deeper to the actual business issues that will make their business objectives reality. The more specific, measurable, and action oriented the marketing goals, the easier it is to apply meaningful metrics to the data we want to analyse and to ultimately know whether the objectives have been met. Most marketers agree that repeat customers cost less to sell to than do new ones (with a few notable exceptions, such as infrequently purchased products or products in categories where post-purchase satisfaction is extremely low).

Customer acquisition is, for many businesses, the most expensive part of the sales cycle, so common sense tells us that any increase in repeat-customer buying should translate straight into a bottom-line increase in profits. If these statements were true in your business, wouldn't you want to measure how prior buyers – rather than the larger set of total visitors or even total purchasers – are using your site and responding to your emails? Not that you wouldn't also study the patterns and behaviours of the larger groups, but if repeat shoppers are your bread and butter, have you set up your analytics to call out that group so you can look at it independently?

Look even closer: Are there apparent subsets within that repeat-shopper segment? Are you reacting and reaching out differently to those who return weekly, as opposed to those who come back annually? Have you tracked the items purchased (or content read or ads viewed for noncommerce sites) by those best customers to figure out how to give them more of what they are looking for? A small incremental purchase from every return customer can, for many businesses, be far more profitable than finding and winning over a first timer. And any change to the site that supports that goal is likely to pay off much more quickly than any customer acquisition effort.

Log analysis programs

WebTrends:	**www.webtrends.com**
FlashStats:	**http://maximized.com/products/flashstats**
Funnel Web:	**www.activeconcepts.com/prod.html**
Analogue:	**www.statslab.cam.ac.uk/~sret1/analog** (free)
Bolero 1.0:	**www.everyware.com**
WebReporter 2.0:	**www.openmarket.com/reporter**
Hit List Professional:	**www.marketwave.com**

APPENDIX

Off-line advertising

Although it is important to market your website on the internet, it is also important to advertise your website off-line.

Advertising

When you think of advertising in the real-world press, consider the price advantage of a small ad, which will drive readers to your web site. The two keys to making a small ad work are:

1 catching the reader's eye
2 intriguing the reader enough to write down your web address.

The first may be accomplished in numerous ways, including colour, stripes, odd shapes, etc. The second may be done by using words and phrases, which make the reader want something, which is found at your web site. For example, if you sell footballs, try a whole series of small ads in a football magazine or tabloid. Put a wide striped border around one, put the copy of another on a picture of a football, and make the third bright yellow with black letters. Use pitches that appeal to different motivations of the reader: 'Tired of paying Full Price for your balls?' 'A Child can kick our balls 300 yards!' Then tell them they'll get something free by visiting your site. 'Check out our balls, and print out a FREE copy of Tony Adam's Guide to becoming a successful football player.'

Be sure to include your URL in any display or classified ads you purchase in trade journals, newspapers, etc. View your website as an information adjunct to the ad. Catch readers' attention with the ad, and then refer them to a web page where they can obtain more information or perhaps place an order. Sometimes these ads are more targeted, more effective, and less expensive than online advertising.

Business stationery

Every company has business cards and official letterheads; most have invoices, envelopes and brochures; some have all sorts of pre-printed promotional material for salespeople to hand out. Everything should have your URL. Every letter, every information packet, every postcard and business card should have your website address. Note that if you have pre-printed pens, mugs, caps or tote bags, it should be on those items as well.

In print, leave off the http:// part and including only the www.domain.com portion.

Free magazine listings

Don't forget that free advertising can be found offline. Look at free computer and internet publications. Occasionally, they offer free classified ad-style website lists or a website of the week feature.

Press releases

Find newsworthy events (such as launching your free service), and send press releases to print and web periodicals in your industry. All you need is a good press release and a list of the right people to send it to. Exposure in magazines, the newspaper, other websites, and on the TV news gives your website more credibility and exposure than the most expensive ad. What's more, this kind of exposure feeds on itself. Even the smallest review could spark another reporter's interest and get your website more exposure.

Write a brief press release up to one page long, including your contact information, a headline, and why their readers or viewers would like to know about your website. How is your website different from the competition? Are you doing something nobody else is? If your website isn't newsworthy, what about your company? Or you?

Include the most important information they will need to write the article like your URL. Put the most important information first; sell the story in the first line of the press release. Find out whom to send it to. Consider local newspapers and newsletters, regional newspapers, local TV stations, local magazines, and national magazines on a topic related to your newsworthiness. Find out which editors you should mail it to and write their names on the envelopes.

Only send your press release to the media catching the visitors you want to come to your site. That doesn't mean you should turn down interviews with other media just because your prospects will never know. Simply spend your time and money wisely.

For websites that do reviews, get their suggestion email addresses and send them all your press release at the same time (BCC addresses or use a list so they can't see who else you sent it to). For the biggest, most important websites, you may want to fill out the form on their website.

Word of mouth advertising

Why would your customers want to talk to their contacts about their experience of doing business with you? What things can you do that will compel them to do so? In order to compel the customers to want to share their good experience, you must make the process memorable, going beyond what is expected. (See also *Let Your Fingers Do the Talking* by Godfrey Harris, Management Books 2000, for some excellent ideas about word-of-mouth on the internet.)

Articles

The internet is the darling of the media at the moment and your web site is a great PR opportunity. Consider articles in the press as well as specialist magazines and ezines. Submitting articles is one of the best free offline and online promotion methods you can use. Write articles that reflect your areas of expertise as seen on your website and include your URL. You can then:

- Send it off to a list of editors who publish material related to what you are marketing. Most magazine and newspaper publishers pay for articles. Some don't, but it might still be worth sending them an article just to generate traffic to your site.
- There are several internet sites that actively seek internet writers to put together online articles in exchange for promoting your site. Email your articles to webmasters and ezine editors.
- Post your articles as stand-alone pages on your own site where they will attract more traffic through the search engines. Make sure each article is keyword rich. Title your article thoughtfully, e.g. the alphabetically strategic first word, the more important words repeated and the hook of the title itself. Also link each article web page back to the home page. Add a page a week or one a month and register it with all the key search engines.

A successful marketing campaign is an integrated one combining online and offline advertising.

This not only leads to a coherent consumer message but will also encourage online and offline sales.

Many teens shop online, buy offline

Nearly one-third of teens research products online before buying them offline, according to new research from Jupiter Media Metrix. The research says that although 89 percent of teens (ages 13-17) have never made an online purchase, 29 percent browse on the web. Jupiter analysts have found that marketers must consider the influence of online window-shopping when developing advertising campaigns and advise companies to incorporate a singular message across multiple ad channels. Jupiter analysts say that companies who want to attract the teenage demographic should allow users to set up and personalise their experience as much as possible. According to a Jupiter Consumer Survey, 42 percent of teenagers view personal web pages set up by other users. Media Metrix ratings data show that homepage providers Angelfire, TriPod and Homestead are all among the top 20 sites visited by teens, though none are among the same list for adults.

Web browsing leads to offline buying

While online sales may not be increasing at the same rate they once were, there is more research that says shoppers are still surfing the web. Ninety-two percent of online consumers use the internet to shop and/or purchase online, according to 'E-Tailers vs. Retailers,' the newest e-Visory report published by leading marketing information provider, the NPD Group. The report shows that even those consumers who aren't making purchases haven't made a purchase online are still influenced by what they see on retailers' web sites. Eighty-four percent of occasional buyers, those who say they have made an online purchase only once in the past six months or less often, describe their usual use of the internet for shopping as 'I usually shop online and go offline to purchase.' 'Measuring online sales alone cannot capture the full benefit of a retailer having an Internet presence. We know that even consumers who don't typically purchase online are using retailers' web sites to browse and decide what to buy,' says Pamela Smith, vice president of NPD online research. 'Although it may not result in a purchase at that time, it could translate directly into an offline sale.'

Web ads effective in driving offline buys

A new survey of British web users shows 78 percent of web users aged 16 to 45 responded in some way to online ads – and not by clicking the ads right off their screens. According to a report from 'The Wall Street Journal Europe,' the study was conducted by media-planning group Starcom Motive Ltd., a unit of Bcom3 Group. For the survey, Starcom focused on people who are internet and tech-savvy. Starcom said the 197 respondents use the internet at least once a week on average. Internet ads in general prompted 38 percent of those interviewed to research a potential purchase online, 34 percent to buy an item on the web and 24 percent to register for a service. One out of 10 people surveyed said internet ads prompted them to buy an item offline.

Video-streaming, superstitials, internet games sponsored by brand names and content sponsorships were formats noted to be well received by the interviewees. Not all the feedback was positive. Eighty-nine percent said they believe the point of online advertising is merely to boost click rates without giving consumers anything back in return. Of those interviewed, 40 percent said internet advertising is intrusive and 51 percent said online ads were always irrelevant to the site they were viewing. Consumers were most turned off by banner ads, especially those designed to look like computer error messages that pop up and ask users to click on them. Pop-up ads tend to prompt a knee-jerk reaction to click them off the screen, users said. And skyscrapers were considered boring, according to the survey.

USEFUL EMAIL NEWSLETTERS FOR MARKETERS

E-mail Marketing News Weekly
www.imarketingnews.com

This is a weekly roundup of the top email marketing stories published at DM News (www.dmnews.com) and iMarketing News.

The eMail Marketing Newsletter
www.emarketer.com

Published weekly by eMarketer.

B2BMarketingBiz
www.marketingsherpa.com

One of MarketingSherpa's channels which publish practical news, case studies, and best practices for corporate marketers, this is both a weekly text ezine and a site with archives of past issues.

Email Marketing News
www.emailmarketingnews.com
> This is both a site and a periodic HTML ezine, dating back to 1998, that covers the email marketing industry.

Opt-in News
www.optinnews.com
> This site is filled with news about permission email marketing, an opt-in discussion forum, an email marketing terminology section, regular columns, and the results of several studies. There is also an industry resource section. You can sign up for the free monthly Opt-in News magazine, delivered as a PDF.

Digitrends.net
www.digitrends.net/marketing/13640.html
> This site has a wealth of news and resources for interactive marketers. You can check out the eMail Marketing section and sign up for Digitrends e-newsletters.

BtoBonline.com
www.netb2b.com
> This is the online version of the tabloid magazine BtoB with lots of stuff specifically related to B2B marketing.

Email Technology Company E-Newsletters
www.constantcontact.com/home.jsp
> Often in HTML to illustrate the company's technology capabilities, these ezines can offer useful information. You can sign up for 'email hints and tips' on Constant Contact by Roving's site.

Ezine-Tips.com
http://ezine-tips.com/about
> If you have a particular interest in e-newsletters as a marketing vehicle, be sure to visit Ezine-Tips.com which also has a daily tips e-newsletter.

VIRAL MARKETING

In the internet age, word of mouth (now renamed 'viral marketing' as coined by Steve Jurvetson) has become an important means of diffusing innovation. For dot-com companies and for traditional business marketing through the web, viral marketing has become the new catch phrase. Once viewed as a renegade approach by those brands without large marketing and PR budgets, it is now accepted industry-wide as a necessary approach to building brand awareness. It's similar in style and approach to that of an off-line guerrilla marketing campaign. The idea is to create a buzz surrounding your product or image. The usual vehicle for the delivery of this message is email, because it can be easily forwarded to a contact either because of a humorous or creative message, or an incentive that has been added to encourage pass-along. Word-of-mouth marketing has to be based on sincerity. You might ignore a million banners advertising a product or service when you surf the web, but you'd try the product in an instant if your best friend gave it a rave review.

The message is, by far, the most important element; without a strong image or enticing copy, a viral message is little more than an irritating email. The easiest type of viral to create is a humorous message, provided that your site, product, or service is not devalued by such an approach. But if you are uncertain about your approach, if it is a new product or service and your advertising budget is small, a humorous message will be worth the risk as well as the brand awareness you wish to attract. A viral message of a pop culture/cutting-edge nature is another effective method. Other items that work well in a viral campaign include strong incentives that appeal to the audience's emotions, or the implementation of quality graphic images. When both or more of the above are combined, however, you'll be leveraging much higher traffic results.

For your viral campaign, you want to send the message to influential people who you believe are trendsetters, and tastemakers. These people can be celebrities, influential members of a particular industry, or ordinary people involved in their communities. They consistently spread word about new things they encounter. Collectively, they have the ability to spark a groundswell of favourable public opinion. According to Malcolm Gladwell in his book, 'The Tipping Point', these people are known as 'Mavens'; according to Seth Godin they are known as 'Sneezers'.

A common practice in the marketing departments of many record labels is to create an internal 'tastemakers' list. The idea is for the department's staff of product managers, vice presidents and marketing associates to combine a list of all of their business associates, friends and colleagues into one database, or the 'tastemakers list'. Basically, this list consists of people who will be most effective at spreading the message of their product, or in this case, creating a buzz about their record. The idea is that the tastemakers will start talking about the single with their industry friends, including DJs and retail buyers, who in turn, determine what consumers listen to and what selections will be available for purchase. Identifying your company's 'Tastemaker's List' will become an important part of your viral and guerrilla campaign.

The mark of a successful campaign is found in the product itself. Eventually, it will be judged on its own merits, compared to the thousands of other available products or services in the industry. This is equally true for your viral message; the foundation is a strong, innovative and creative idea. Eventually both forms will have to survive on their own, outside of any promotional efforts. Therefore, its message must be likeable, innovative and catchy enough to hook people from just one listen, as a viral message must do from just one read.

Examples of viral marketing

Hotmail (before the Microsoft acquisition) is a classic example. It grew by leaps and bounds by doing something simple: At the bottom of each e-mail message, there was a small line promoting Hotmail-'Get Your Private, Free Email at www.hotmailcom'. The recipient of the message quickly understood that he could get an account quickly and easily by visiting Hotmail. This led to phenomenal growth - more than 12 million people signed up in the first year and a half. Hotmail had spent only $500,000 on marketing and promotion during this period-an acquisition cost of about 4 cents per customer.

Real-time chat service ICQ (short for 'I seek you') signed up 12 million users by taking viral marketing one step further. In order to enable chat between friends, each person had to have the service. People signed up their friends and ICQ eventually sold out to AOL for about $300 million.

Viral marketing is not for everybody and every situation. From a strategic standpoint, it's called for when you care only about the quantity rather than the quality of traffic. It works best when you're interested in getting a lot of people to do something and you're not choosy about who these people are. It also works well when you want a homogeneous slice of the market, e.g. teenagers. Viral marketing works best for products or services that has one or more of the following characteristics:

Uniqueness   Viral marketing is applicable for products or services that are nothing like what's available in the market and that represents a new way of thinking. Consider Hotmail. At the point of its launch, most e-mail providers charged a flat service fee. Providing free e-mail represented a new way of thinking. Today, people take free e-mail for granted and launching a free e-mail service will not get you results.

Low trial cost   When a consumer receives a message, if he has to try the product, the total cost of adopting the product must be low. The total cost of adoption can be broken down into several components-switching costs e.g. the cost of learning a new product/technology, price of the product and transaction cost. The best viral campaigns are for a free product and are very easy to pass on to others.

Simple product concept   If a consumer has to explain what a product is to his or her friend, neighbour or acquaintance, you can make their work easier if the product is simple. Remember Hotmail. The concept was simple and could be described in two words 'Free e-mail'.

Exciting product concept   In viral marketing, success depends on individuals passing on the message to others. They will only do so if they're excited with the product or service and the value proposition. Therefore, it's great for products or services that are entertaining and colourful to the user.

MORE USEFUL LINKS

Search Engine Colossus
www.searchenginecolossus.com/
   The ultimate collection of links to every known search engine anywhere in the world!

Submit it!
www.submit-it.com/
   The Leader in quick submission

The Informant
www.webpromotion.co.uk/link.htm&frame2=http://informant.dartmouth.edu
Can monitor search engines for you and notify you by e-mail when a new instance of a search term is found.

http://ezinesearch.com
Use this site to search for ezines on your area of expertise. Email editors and ask them if they accept article submissions.

UltraEdit-32
www.idmcomp.com/products/index.html
An ASCII based word processing program offering features for those publishing email newsletters or discussion groups.

Mailloop
www.mailloop.com
Designed as a bulk email program. Demo version is available for free download.

CyberCount
www.cybercount.com/
Free hit-counter and visitor tracking system.

Gumball Tracker
www.gumball-tracker.com/
Gumball is an invisible website tracker that allows webmasters to create unique, website traffic reports to their own specifications. Reliable, invisible, password protected, unlimited pages.

Europages Link Resources
www.webpromotion.co.uk/resourcelinks.htm
Use this to find complimentary companies to target for links. Has nice ability to find online businesses sorted by sector.

Zebulon: Exchange of Links
www.fraternt.com/zel/zel6.htm
An announcement forum among (email) subscribers.

WEBpromotion.co.uk
www.webpromotion.co.uk/
Hundreds of links, articles, tools, news and views on web site promotion.

Virtual Promote Awards
www.virtualpromote.com/hotsites.html
> Links to some of the most important award sites on the internet and masses of extra information.

Adam J Boettiger's I-Advertising Digest
www.internetadvertising.org/
> A moderated, global discussion group on internet advertising, marketing and online commerce.

Newsgroups:
alt.business
misc.entrepreneurs
biz.marketplace
aol.commerce.mim.announce

www.PRweb.com
www.webaware.co.uk/netset/text
> You can submit press releases through these free press release services.

Search engine sites:
www.altavista.com
www.askjeeves.com
www.directhit.com
www.dmoz.org
www.excite.com
www.go.com
www.google.com
www.hotbot.com
www.iwon.com
www.looksmart.com
www.lycos.com
www.msn.com
www.netscape.com
www.northernlight.com
www.snap.com
www.webcrawler
www.yahoo.com

List Resources.com
http://list-resources.com
A directory of sites that list newsletters and ezines.

Advertising Standards Authority
www.asa.org.uk/
The ASA aims to promote the highest standards in advertising. It does this by a programme of industry information and training through some 70 presentations and seminars each year.

AFD Postcodes and ADF ZipAddresses
www.afd.co.uk (postcode information)
www.zipaddress.com (zip address information)
These two programs use software that generates full addresses from only the postcode – you just add the street number or house name. The PostCode version covers the UK. ZipAddress all the US zipcodes with over 100 million addresses. It also has a built-in one-off label printing facility and a PostNet barcode font.

Electronic Yellow Pages
www.eyp.co.uk/
Here you will find an easy-to-use directory claiming 1.6 million-plus classified businesses around the UK.

Hollis UK Press and Public Relations Annual
www.hollis-pr.co.uk
Link into publications, PR consultancies, contacts and services.

Internet Directory Enquiries
www.internet192.com/
Over 1.4. million listings can be accessed through this site, which includes an A-Z of business types.

Media UK Directory
www.mediauk.com/directory/
This site offers a detailed directory of UK media sites on the internet.

Thomson Directories INbusiness
www.inbusiness.co.uk
A comprehensive online directory of businesses in Britain.

Adam J Boettiger's I-Advertising Digest

www.internetadvertising.org/

Link into a moderated, global discussion group on internet advertising, marketing and online commerce.

Article submission

www.web-source.net/articlesub.htm

www.ideamarketers.com/

You can automate the submission of articles to ezines through both these sites.

Business 2.0

www.business2.com/

An ecommerce business directory aimed at the hi-tech executive. Categories include advertising, finance, general news, and market research.

E-commerce Awards Scheme

www.isi-interforum-awards.com

The Awards celebrate and reward UK small and medium sized companies, which have been successful in doing business electronically.

eCommerce Weekly

www.eweekly.com/

eCommerce Weekly (formerly Entrepreneur Weekly) is a free weekly newsletter designed to bring you the latest online sales, marketing, and ecommerce strategies to help you succeed online. In addition, they bring you the latest news of companies and services geared to helping internet entrepreneurs do business on the net.

Ezines

http://ezinesearch.com

http://list-resources.com

Search for ezines and newsletters on your area of expertise. Email editors and ask them if they accept article submissions.

The Marketing Resource Center

www.marketingsource.com/

The Marketing Resource Center is designed to assist businesses with their traditional and internet marketing efforts.

Virtual Promote Awards
www.virtualpromote.com/hotsites.html

Visit the links to some of the most important award sites on the internet and masses of extra information.

Web Marketing Today
www.wilsonweb.com/wmt/

Link into a free twice-monthly electronic newsletter about internet marketing and doing business on the web.

Online Customer Relationship Management (CRM)

Your goal is lots of satisfied customers – happy ones who become loyal, repeat buyers as well as active referrers. But just because they bought from you once doesn't mean you have a relationship with them. In fact, for all you know, they're not coming back, and maybe for a very good reason. So you need to create an online shopping experience that plants the seeds of a real relationship. Then, you have to nurture those seeds with outstanding fulfilment and customer service.

One of the most overlooked aspects of any CRM strategy is the people on each end of the equation. We talk about being customer focused, but to what extent do we think that purchasing software to help manage relationships will make us so? And to what extent do we think we can rely on the existing skills that employees have to execute on a CRM strategy? The point is that value in the relationship is based on the input from each person involved. The tool should enable that relationship, not develop it all by itself. Here are some of the skills necessary for better managing relationships with online customers:

- Correctly delivering products and services to customers requires correlating customer needs with the products and services available. Whether you are selling chemicals or infrastructure services, make sure those who are managing CRM efforts are well versed in both marketing and products.
- Whether your CRM efforts are focused on customer service, personalisation, merchandising, or marketing messaging, defining what is the right communication to a specific customer under specific circumstances is a challenge.

- Don't expect a piece of software to solve all your CRM challenges. Even if software dynamically segments users, you still need to define attributes and build predictive models. While many tools on the market offer clustering and segmentation capabilities, it helps to have those tools used by people experienced in analysing data, developing segmentation models, and defining customer attributes.
- A core objective of most CRM efforts is to increase the success of customer-acquisition efforts or to reduce the cost of such efforts. While employees with direct marketing backgrounds are usually a good fit for that task, challenge those employees to transcend the calculating tactics of direct marketing by integrating best practices from that realm with those of long-term customer life cycle planning. Encourage employees to think of each interaction with the customer as adding a building block, not making a sale.

No one expects those working in the CRM realm to have spent years in IT learning how to develop applications or design system architecture. However, understanding how technology works and its limitations, and how it can be used in the context of the entire organisation, is a critical skill. Finding people with such a mixed skill set (technical and marketing savvy) can be challenging, but having people in charge of CRM who don't have a technical competency will likely create more challenges. Also, look for people who understand how to use the internet to deliver products and services to customers. Not all things should be delivered via the web, and not all interactions should occur on the web. All too often, features are built because it is possible to build them – not because there is a need or demand for them. Make sure that those responsible for your CRM efforts understand the difference and can demonstrate the impact of certain features on customer relationships.

Some of the most common web site weaknesses in the area of customer relations include:

- Visitors are usually required to type out complaints.
- The site may be 'Temporarily Unavailable' or download slowly.
- There is slowness or failure to respond to customer inquiries.
- Customer service capabilities may be confusing. The right contacts may be hard to find. Or only a general email addresses, or addresses for webmasters may be offered.
- There is reluctance to give visitors access to people in authority.
- Customer service personnel may not be competent or helpful.

- There is lack of face-to-face contact. Some matters can be more easily explained in person.
- Customer service may be hard to reach.

Jupiter Media Metrix (**www.jmm.com**), a global market intelligence giant, based in New York City, recently published some revealing findings concerning online customer service, especially as it pertains to the growing 'click-and-mortar' sites – those that operate both online and offline, and which represent a growing share of dominant online operations. For instance, the study found that click-and-mortar retailers that provide inadequate online customer service might see as many as 70 percent of buyers spending less money at their offline stores. The report also reveals that only 18 percent of click-and-mortar retailers are capable of accessing a customer's consolidated account activity across all sales and service channels (online and offline). Jupiter analysts advise click-and-mortar retailers to integrate their CRM capabilities in order to retain customer relationships and meet consumer demand. Some of Jupiter's major survey findings were:

- Sixty-seven percent of online buyers expect store staff to be able to view their online account information. Jupiter analysts found that retailers should be using browser-based CRM applications that allow store staff to act as remote customer service representatives with access to consumer data across all channels.
- Eighty-three percent of online buyers want to be able to return online purchases at offline stores, and 59 percent said that they would like to order products online, and pick them up at offline stores. (Jupiter found only 18 percent of multichannel retailers offer this capability). Jupiter analysts say that non-integrated product inventory is a major cause of customer dissatisfaction with online service. Therefore, they believe, there's only limited opportunity for companies that automate returns processing for online-only retailing.

John Tschohl, president of Minneapolis-based Service Quality Institute says of Jupiter's findings. 'Business and consumers want speed, technology and price built around service. Many firms that are totally dependent on the internet will go out of business when they run out of marketing and advertising money to acquire new customers.' The most common mistake that web sites make, according to Tschohl, is to hire the wrong people for customer relations. 'Internet firms hire techies who do everything they can to avoid communicating with customers because they're uncomfortable,' he says. 'These people are process and analytically driven, and are poor on people skills. Web sites also frequently use CRM software that's not sensitive to customer needs. If a supermarket had 98 percent of loaded shopping carts abandoned, the store manager would be fired immediately. This happens every day on the internet, where 98 percent of shopping carts are abandoned at checkout.' Online follow-up, Tschohl adds, is another major problem. 'Most firms would return phone calls,' he points out. 'But the Jupiter report shows 29 percent of companies don't return e-mails, which is the same as a phone call. They need to understand that online customers are less forgiving.'

Tschohl's useful tips:

1. Buy books on customer service and training programs.
2. Respond to all e-mails within 60 minutes.
3. Recruit people who love customers and have people skills.
4. Train all employees in the art of service, starting with you. Introduce new customer service training programs every six months.
5. Update your web site daily and weekly.
6. Disclose pricing and create a shopping cart so people can buy your offerings online.
7. Make it easy for people to do business with you.
8. Every web site should list a free number.

Companies looking to improve customer loyalty, reduce customer acquisition costs and increase sales need to broaden their ideas of CRM and look for better ways to measure their customers' behaviour. Online research firm Jupiter Media Metrix says companies focusing more on viral marketing and customer satisfaction can improve customer loyalty and reduce customer acquisition costs by 27 percent, as well as increase average order sizes by up to 60 percent.

According to a Jupiter Consumer Survey, 45 percent of online shoppers choose e-commerce web sites based on word-of-mouth recommendations, but a mere 7 percent of companies are using tools to enable them to measure viral e-mail campaigns. 'Most companies are not tracking their customers' behaviour adequately enough to understand customer loyalty,' says David Daniels, analyst for Jupiter Media Metrix. 'Businesses need to identify what influences their customers purchasing decisions and they should tart by building a broader view of consumer behaviour. While no single CRM application currently offers a comprehensive view of a company's customers, some wise businesses have devised methods to do so and have experienced a drastic reduction in acquisition costs and significant increases in average order sizes.'

Jupiter's research found most companies focus merely on the monetary metrics when identifying loyal customers and don't focus on customer-satisfaction scores, thus alienating loyal customers who may spend less-per-purchase but will continue to frequent the site. By utilising e-mail, companies can better track and measure pass-along rates and develop better loyalty campaigns.

Jupiter advice for multichannel retailers:

- Move customer service operations in-house where it's easier to manage integration processes. Cut costs... by outsourcing infrastructure and deploying hosted CRM applications that allow business managers to focus on customers and staff.
- Leverage browser-based CRM applications that allow store managers to add comments to customer service history, and help build one cross-channel view of customer's transactions.
- Incorporate stringent customer service quality inspection measures, including call monitoring and customer satisfaction scoring.

The following metrics categories can help you diagnose symptoms of poor customer support:

- Shopping cart abandonment
- Email queue volume
- Call center volume
- Conversion rates
- Slower response times

Truly customer-friendly organisations make the customer experience a high priority. They build e-commerce sites around the customer's shopping and buying process, not the organisation's process for selling stuff to unwary consumers. Similarly, they build web sites based on users' needs for information, not the need to boost upper management's egos. Users know when they've landed on a site that screams 'I'm the big I am but I don't know how to run a user-friendly website' Those are the sites with the dancing graphics, columns of self-congratulatory content, and photos of big buildings or very important vice presidents (count how many times you see the words 'synergy,' 'next level,' and 'proactive'). Missing in action on bigIam.com are basic consumer information, easy-to-navigate pages, and a way to contact a live person. If you want your site to say 'customer friendly,' consider the following:

- Test for Uncle Fred. Test your site on someone so lacking in web savvy that he can barely click a mouse (such as Uncle Fred). Watch him as he navigates the site, and listen to him if he gets frustrated.
- Listen and tweak. Few things are perfect for their trial runs, so expect to tweak as you get more customer feedback. Brushing off that one angry complainer as just a 'whiner' or a 'wacko' could be a mistake.
- Leave your computer terminal every once in a while and actually talk to people. It could be the most effective and cheapest CRM activity you do all year.
- Don't be the lone CRM advocate. Even the most customer-friendly site must be supported by a customer-friendly organisation. There are times when consumers want to talk to someone, so watch out if your call centre is rude or puts people on hold. The idea is to have the site reflect a company-wide customer-welcoming attitude.
- Beware of focus groups. Companies are spending wildly to fund focus groups for marketing programs and product testing. Most of the time, it makes a lot of sense. But people in focus groups also perform for those behind the mirrored window and for each other. Put a non-techie in the room with a bunch of techno fiends, and he or she will never tell you the frustrations experienced by a less-than-savvy user.

Every company understands the competitive value of superior customer service; however, many companies underestimate the level of effort and resources required to keep customers happy throughout the entire relationship cycle. Like any other operation, customer support should be evaluated in terms of its impact on overall company performance. Here is a guide that will help you make decisions related to CRM:

- Web is cheaper than email. Email is cheaper than phone. Savvy e-commerce sites sparingly use call centers as a line of support.
- Speed matters. Reaction time is one of the greatest determinants of high customer satisfaction.

- Help customers help themselves. Self-help is the most cost-effective customer support tactic. E-commerce sites that provide thorough instructional pages or contextual FAQs improve transaction conversion rates and reduce user frustration.
- Understand the cost structure of each communication channel. Each customer contact point is associated with a price. Developing a cost profile of each channel can help you evaluate where to invest the pounds.
- It's never perfect. Customer support should be viewed as the lifework of an enterprise. A commitment to continual improvement should be driven from executive leaders of a company.

Knowledge of corporate product and service offerings

Correctly delivering products and services to customers requires correlating customer needs with the products and services available. Whether you are selling chemicals or infrastructure services, make sure those who are managing CRM efforts are well versed in both marketing and products.

FURTHER READING

Secrets of Profitable E-commerce, Laurel Alexander, Management Books 2000

101 Ways to Get Great Publicity, Timothy R V Foster, Kogan Page

How to Do your Own Advertising, Michael Bennie, How To Books

Marketing your Business on the Internet, Sara Edlington, Internet Handbooks

The Daily Telegraph's Electronic Business Manual, Net Profit

Index